THE
HEATHER
ISLES

THE HEATHER ISLES

A JOURNEY THROUGH THE OUTER
HEBRIDES

Bruce Sandison

with photographs by Michael Hockney

UNWIN HYMAN

First published in Great Britain by the Trade Division
of Unwin Hyman Limited, 1990

UNWIN HYMAN LIMITED
15–17 Broadwick Street
London W1V 1FP

Allen & Unwin Australia Pty Ltd
8 Napier Street, North Sydney, NSW 2060, Australia

Allen & Unwin New Zealand Pty Ltd with the Port
Nicholson Press
Compusales Building, 75 Ghuznee Street, Wellington,
New Zealand

**British Library Cataloguing in
Publication Data**
Sandison, Bruce
    The heather isles.
    1. Scotland. Western Isles, History
    I. Title
    941.1'4
      ISBN 0-04-0440424-7

Designed by Jonathan Newdick
Filmset by August Filmsetting, Haydock, St Helens
Origination by Tenson and Polert Ltd, Hong Kong
Printed by Colorcraft Ltd

Kismul Castle, Barra, ancient home of Clan Macneil

CONTENTS

For Ann

I fell in love with the 'Heather Isles' many years ago, when we spent a glorious family holiday on North Uist, Benbecula and South Uist. I have returned frequently to the islands ever since, captivated by the magic spell that ensnares all who make the rough journey across the broken waters of the Minch to the 'the islands on the edge of the world'.

This book describes my most recent visit to the 'Long Island' and I have tried to capture some of the special charm and unique character of these lovely islands. The principal difficulty facing anyone writing about the Outer Hebrides lies in trying to find adequate words to describe the scenery. I have tried as best as I can, but the real answer is to go and see for yourself. If you do, then, like me, you will be trapped forever by their beauty.

Mike Hockney's wonderful photographs give an indication of what awaits the visitor and I have been delighted to collaborate with such an outstanding photographer in the production of this volume. His magnificent photographs vividly illustrate and enliven my text.

The title of the book, *The Heather Isles*, is perhaps not entirely correct since that name is most often applied to the island of Lewis, rather than to the whole group. If this offends some, then I beg their forgiveness; but I have always thought of the Outer Hebrides in these terms and that is how they appear to me.

The Heather Isles follows a long tradition of descriptive accounts of the Hebrides, dating as far back as the sixteenth century when Dean Munro started the trend by describing his journey in 1594. Martin Martin in 1697, Johnson and Boswell during the late eighteenth century, and countless others have all been bewitched by the wild Hebrides and I have relied upon their work and the work of others to help me along my way.

If some of my impressions and stories differ from your own experiences then I apologize: we all see things in different ways but I have tried, to the best of my ability, to be as accurate as possible. Practical details about getting to the islands may be obtained from the Outer Hebrides Tourist Board, 4 South Beach Street, Stornoway, Isles of Lewis, PA87 2XY, Scotland, telephone: (0851) 3088/2941. For information on getting to St Kilda, contact: The Nature Conservancy Council, Fraser Darling House, 9 Culduthel Road, Inverness, IV2 4AG, Scotland, telephone: (0463) 239431.

As always, I am indebted to my publisher, Merlin Unwin, whose unfailing support and encouragement during the writing of this book has been wonderful: coping with my tantrums and delays with his customary courtesy and patience. I am also grateful to my wife, Ann, who has given me great critical help with the text, hopefully enabling me to avoid some of the disasters I so often manage to create for myself.

Finally, I would like to thank the people of the Hebrides themselves, from the Butt of Lewis to Barra, for their gentle courtesy and for the warm welcome they always extend to visitors. Their kindness makes a journey through the Outer Hebrides an absolute joy; and I am grateful for the privilege of spending so many happy hours in their splendid company, and in their beautiful land.

RUTHER HOUSE
WATTEN
CAITHNESS

JANUARY 1989

1
LEWIS

ULLAPOOL TO STORNOWAY,
BALALLAN AND GARYNAHINE

I sailed from Ullapool to Stornoway on a warm, September afternoon; and as the Saturday loading-bustle of cars and lorries bumped aboard, their weight nudged the ship gently against the quay, making her impatient to be gone. Late arrivals hurried along the jetty; fathers and mothers clutching bags and babies, herding over-excited children up the gangplank.

The slow throb of the engines increased as lines were cast off. Then, free at last, the MV *Hebrides* moved slowly astern, propellers churning a white-foamed arc, heading out into the calm, cold waters of Loch Broom; the familiar, comforting feel of a ship moving under my feet. Twenty-five foreign fishing vessels, factory-ships, lay at anchor in Broom Roads and Annat Bay; grey, marine multi-storey towers, clouded with squabbling crowds of seagulls. 'Klondikers', exploiting fish from the rich waters of the west.

A vast, double rainbow arched over the bay, framing the mountains of Inverpolly and Assynt: Ben More Coigach, towering over Isle Martin; Cul Mor, Cul Beag and Stack Polly. Suilven, the Viking's 'Pillar Mountain'; Quinag, 'the Spout', guarding Kylesku; and Sutherland's highest peak, mighty Ben More Assynt.

Northwards, the scattered shapes of the Summer Isles lazed in the late afternoon sunlight; shades and shadows, glimmering green, blue and black. Southwards, the fang of An Teallach, 'the forge', sprang majestically from the Fisherfield Forest; in distant Flowerdale, towered Slioch, 'the Spear' and Liathach, 'the Grey One'.

As we cleared Greenstone Point the long spine of the Trotternish Ridge on the misty island of Skye filled the horizon, the Old Man of Storr, a stark pinnacle, etched black against the molten silver of evening seas. Seagulls screamed overhead and my first gannet slip-streamed astern, dipping and swooping, snow-white and yellow breasted on black-tipped wings.

A tall, bearded young man stood next to me, watching the fading shapes of the Klondikers. He was dressed for hiking and scrabbled in his rucksack for a camera: 'Just amazing' he said, snapping happily. 'Yes' I replied. 'Princes Street on a Saturday

Stornoway — a busy fishing port with an air of prosperity quite unlike that of other Hebridean communities

One of Stornoway's many drinking houses – but never on Sunday

night, but they bring a lot of money to the north.' He gave me a puzzled look: 'No, I don't mean the factory-ships, I mean the view. I've never seen anything so beautiful.'

Given the number of people that I had watched boarding, the decks were strangely deserted. Perhaps the locals were over-familiar with the view. A few visitors, like myself, stood wedged into corners, feet braced against the swell, waiting out the lingering evening; spell-bound, reluctant to lose a moment of the magnificent panorama of mountains and sea.

Salt-spray flew from the bow as the vessel met the thrust of the broken waters of the Minch. Light faded. Ahead and astern, bright lights blinked stuttered warning messages from buoys and points. Darkness settled and it began to rain. Fine, cold droplets searching my face and neck, sending me hurrying below, seeking warmth and shelter. Which is where I found, or rather heard, my missing fellow passengers – in the bar.

One hundred Gaelic voices singing. Haunting melodies, rising and falling to the lift and plunge of the ship, as she dipped and rolled her way westwards over the Minch towards Lewis, the 'Heather Isles' of the Outer Hebrides. Islanders returning from the 'Mod' in Glasgow – the annual festival and celebration of Gaelic culture. I found a chair by the door and sat listening and watching with pleasure and amazement. Song after song in perfect harmony, loud and rousing then soft and romantic. A piper played, fanning the fierce tinder pride that lies in every Highland heart.

Tables were covered with bottles and full glasses: whisky, gin, brandy, vodka and rum. The bar, six-deep then, was getting busier by the minute. Red-faced staff worked at lightning speed. A man rose, unsteadily from his seat: 'Now, are you all right on your own, dear?' asked his wife solicitously, as he staggered out.

The choir was in full flood and two young men stood chatting near to where I sat: 'Are you still standing, Duncan?' asked one. 'Oh, aye, barely,' replied the other, 'but I'll be rolling before the night's out.'

'Home is the sailor,
home from the sea.'
Stornoway Harbour

Feeding time at Enaclete

The saloon was divided fore and aft by a partition and, resting his head against it, as though asleep, a handsome young man lazed, legs outstretched, eyes closed, seemingly oblivious to the mirth around him. As the choir ended and the company roared approval, he began to sing, quietly, eyes still closed. Those nearest fell silent first. Then, like a white mist enfolding a blue, distant mountain, the silence grew. Until all that could be heard was his single, clear, timeless voice, rising above the noise of the engines and cascading waves, fleeing urgently astern.

I held my breath, trapped by the mystical sound. The silence was complete; and long after the song had ended, as though to capture the moment forever, silence remained. Then, spontaneous, rapturous, delighted applause. The young man slumbered on.

I left the saloon and went back on deck. A full moon spilled its white light from between silver-edged clouds, washing foam-fringed waves as they swept by. Off the starboard bow, Tumpan Head Light on the Eye Peninsula winked welcome. Rain danced on the

decks, keeping time to the music below.

The ferry nosed carefully between Holm and Arnish Points into the calm waters of Stornoway Harbour and the lights of the town greeted us, growing ever brighter. Black shapes took on meaning; houses, church, wet shining streets, small, rain-soaked figures waiting for our arrival on the pier. As we came alongside, the party below decks ended with a last song and a final cheer. Bagpipes and piano accordions were put away. Sudden stillness, then, fading chatter as people made their way to the car-deck and landing stage. I glanced round the deserted saloon. Nothing but empty glasses. Not a single drop of liquid left anywhere.

Lewis is the largest of the Outer Hebridean Isles and with its neighbour, Harris, extends for a distance of nearly sixty miles: from the Butt of Lewis in the north to Renish Point near the tiny village of Rodel on Harris in the south. At its greatest breadth, the island touches the Atlantic at Aird Uig in the west, and twenty miles east,

Sharing a lift to the lazy-beds

Callanish — a mighty symphony in stone

probes the Minch with fjord-like fingers in the ancient parish of Pairc.

Wild, desolate, peat moorlands cover most of Lewis; to the north, low lying, bog-wet and treacherous. Southwards, rising to the craggy peaks of Mealisval, Cracaval and Tahaval above the white sands of Uig; and eastwards, to Beinn Mhor, Muait-habhal and Carn Ban, by Loch Seaforth in the Parish of Lochs.

People have lived in these distant lands on the edge of the Atlantic for thousands of years. The Standing Stones of Callanish are a great, prehistoric hymn to their endeavours; Neolithic settlers, forced by unknown circumstances from Europe, trekking north-wards in search of food, peace and security.

Lewis abounds with the evidence of their passing: standing stones, circles, burial chambers, earth houses and homesteads, cran-nogs, duns and brochs. A record of uninterrupted habitation stretching back for almost 7,000 years. A history that is still largely unexplored and only vaguely understood; so many unanswered questions, guarded secrets, covered by time in endless layers of dark island peat and white, machair sands.

Few of these settlers found the peace and security for which they were searching, for the history of Lewis is a story of the continual subjugation of the inhabitants by a succession of self-seeking, ruth-less invaders, almost down to the present time.

From the numbers of fortified dwellings scattered throughout the

The stark outline of St Molua's Church, Eoropie Teampull

Required reading in Lewis. These original texts are still used by Ministers today

OVERLEAF *Stone Circle at Garynahine*

One of the two kirks at Miavaig

island, it is obvious that earning one's daily Neolithic bread was a precarious affair. Druids and early Christian missionaries battled for the islanders' souls. The Vikings used the Outer Hebrides, and their people, as little other than a larder for supplies of food and slaves.

Clan rivalry and the political birth of Scotland as a nation made life on the Outer Hebrides very uncertain for centuries during the Middle Ages; choosing which side to support could mean the difference between life and death. Even once it became possible to go to sleep at night with the reasonable certainty of waking up in one's own bed, rather than being interviewed by St Peter, just trying to live was still hard and fraught with difficulties.

Omnipotent lairds ruled the land with a rod of iron; using its scant resources largely for their own profit and pleasure. When those resources failed to live up to their expectations, the poor inhabitants were forced to make up the difference; regardless of their own simple needs or the requirements of their families.

From 1843 onwards, the Disruption of the Church of Scotland and the formation of the Free Church, compounded the islanders' problems. Whilst the lairds still wanted the bodies and labours of the islanders to fill their coffers, the Free Church ministers were even more demanding and overpowering. They required nothing less than the minds and hearts of the people for their stern, Calvinistic God.

Throughout history, there has always seemed to be someone, self-righteous or otherwise, willing, ready and anxious to tell the people of the Hebrides how they should lead their lives: what they should do or should not do; how they should think, work, play and pray. Down the ages, advice has arrived, endlessly, either on the point of a sword or in carefully-couched civil service jargonese, mostly to be forced down unwilling throats. Advice from Iona, Norway, Dunvegan, Inverness, Edinburgh, London and now Brussels.

That the islanders, in the face of this never-ending flood of instruction and advice, have managed to retain their identity, sanity and pride, speaks volumes for the Hebridean character; welcoming but cautious, slow to anger, but determined in adversity, independent and self-sufficient where it matters most – in their minds.

Donald Macdonald, in his fine book *Lewis: A History of the Island*, quotes a statement made by Lord Leverhulme, who, in the 1920s, tried to do much to benefit the island's economy, and it aptly describes the Lewis character:

> I cannot claim a thorough knowledge of the average Lewisman, but I am firmly convinced on a few points; first that they are a very fine people, and that I am very fond of them, notwithstanding that they are a little difficult at times; the next is, that you may lead a Lewisman with a hair, but you won't drag him with a cable.

I drove into Stornoway, 'Anchor Bay' to the Vikings, at about 9.30 that evening, windscreen wipers working overtime, rain coming down in sheets. The ferry terminal and east side of the harbour is the oldest part of the town, lined with fine stone buildings giving an air of prosperity, quite unlike other Hebridean communities I know.

The town has a population of about 5,000 and is the main commercial and administrative centre for the Outer Hebrides. Stornoway was, and still is, an important fishing port, and for centuries sailors have found shelter in its fine, natural harbour; protected by the twin 'islands' of the Eye Peninsula, northwards, and the crooked arm of Arnish Point to the south.

The Dutch, pre-eminent fishermen of the sixteenth century, knew Stornoway Harbour and were so successful in their herring fishing that, in 1603, King James VI of Scotland (James I of England) invited a group of prominent Lowland Scots, known as the Fife Adventurers (including Lord Balmerino, Sir James Spence and Sir George Hay) to establish and develop a Scottish fishery in the port. James VI also hoped that by settling more 'civilized' Lowlanders in the Hebrides, he would bring his unruly, constantly feuding, island subjects to heel. In both instances, he was disap-

Outstanding value – many of the crofters have looms, advertizing their home-made tweed on the roadside

View to the magnificent Eilean Molach, Mangersta, near Uig

pointed. The traditional lairds, the Macleods, opposed every move and although Neil Macleod was eventually caught and banished to Holland, the Fife Adventurers returned to the 'Wee Kingdom' with their tails between their legs.

The entrance to Stornoway harbour can be hard to find in wild weather and on 1 January 1919 a terrible disaster struck the island, devastating almost every family. The vessel, HMY *Iolaire*, returning from Kyle of Lochalsh with sailor survivors of the First World War, failed to find the harbour entrance and in huge seas, at 1.55 in the morning, ran aground on the Brests of Holm, just off Arnish Point. The *Iolaire* overturned and quickly sank a few yards from the shore, leaving little time to launch lifeboats. Two hundred and six men drowned on that awful night.

That seventy-nine souls survived the wreck was largely due to the outstanding courage of John Macleod, a native of Port of Ness. He managed to make the perilous journey ashore, carrying a line, and pulled a hawser to the rocks along which his fellow sailors scrambled to safety.

Lewismen have paid dearly for Britain's wars at other times too, and its famous regiment, the Seaforth Highlanders, raised in 1778 by the laird Kenneth McKenzie, has fought Britain's battles all over the world. The regiment served first in India where it gained the name 'Saviours of India' during the Mutiny; Colin Mackenzie, a Lewisman, became the first Surveyor General of that country.

The Seaforths also fought against Napoleon in Italy and Egypt and in the Crimean campaign and Boer Wars. During the Great War, hundreds of Lewismen died in the nightmare mire of the Flanders trenches; and throughout the carnage of the Second World War, the island suffered heavily for its loyalty to King and Country.

For generations, the highlands and islands of Scotland supplied the Crown with 'cannon fodder'. After Bonnie Prince Charlie's abortive 1745 Rebellion, rapacious, glory-seeking lairds, backed by successive governments, encouraged the raising of Highland regiments. It served the dual purpose of breaking the clan system and keeping the ever-hungry ranks of the army full.

Highlanders were coerced by their lairds, and often their ministers, to accept the 'King's Shilling'. There was little choice because to refuse meant almost certain eviction from their homes. The infamous press gang marched men off to the navy in the late eighteenth century and those soldiers and sailors who were not killed, often returned home only to find that the factor had evicted their families anyway, leaving them destitute and defenceless.

Even after the Great War, when Lewismen came home to a supposed 'land fit for heroes', they had to fight their laird for the right to farm the lands of their ancestors. Whilst the Crofters Act of 1886 gave existing tenants security of tenure, it did nothing to help the thousands who had already been evicted; and when Lord Leverhulme bought Lewis in 1917, he was ill-prepared for the strength of feeling expressed by the Great War veterans.

The Land Raids of 1919 and the early 1920s divided the people of Lewis. Leverhulme, a true philanthropist, was spending £200,000 each year in his various schemes to improve island life; principally to encourage fishing, which he saw as the best hope for the future prosperity of the 'long isle'. He found it difficult to understand the deeply-felt desire of the servicemen to practise subsistence farming on tiny pockets of poor land which he wanted to retain in large units in order to supply milk to the expanding town of Stornoway, rather than having to depend upon importing it from mainland Scotland. Their differing views proved to be irreconcilable, and, eventually, even the Scottish Office, for various, suspicious reasons, supported the land-hungry soldiers. In a welter of accusation and recrimination, all Leverhulme's schemes were abandoned, and the men got the land they wanted.

There is no doubt that Lord Leverhulme's intentions were highly honourable, which is probably far more than could be said for the intentions of some previous owners of the island. It has been said of Leverhulme: 'The ruling passion of his life was not money or even power, but the desire to increase human well-being.'

True to his belief, when Lord Leverhulme left Lewis, in the early 1920s, he bequeathed much of the island to a newly formed group, the Stornoway Trust, which still flourishes to this day — Lewis' only Leverhulme memorial.

I drove through Stornoway, yellow street lights illuminating closed shop windows, peering through the storm, trying to make out the Gaelic names on signposts. Lews Castle College, surrounded by dark trees, loomed across the little river to my left; built by Sir James Matheson, who bought Lewis in 1844 for £190,000, out of money made from his tea-planting 'empire' in Asia. He built schools and roads throughout the island; including playing a major role in the establishment of that famous Scottish educational centre of excellence, the Stornoway Nicolson Institute. Sir James also spent money improving Stornoway harbour, encouraging fishing.

James Shaw Grant, editor of *The Stornoway Gazette*, in his delightful book *Surprise Island*, tells much about the early days of the Stornoway Nicolson Institute and one of its most famous and successful rectors, W. J. Gibson, appointed in 1894. During his long 'reign', 'Gibby' as he was affectionately known, saw 250 of his pupils enter university: 'more than 90 per cent of them having come from Gaelic-speaking homes in the rural villages.' So much for 'the rude speech of a barbarous people' as claimed by the Society in Scotland for the Propagation of Christian Knowledge.

Stornoway is also the centre of the Harris Tweed Industry which earns the islands an annual income of £20m and provides much needed employment throughout the Hebrides. The Globe trademark, taken from the armorial bearings of the Dunmore family, has become world famous and it is jealously guarded and protected by the industry.

The development and growth of spinning and weaving on the islands was much encouraged by Mrs Mackenzie of Dunmore, who brought the spinning wheel to the Long Isles and acted as an un-paid public relations officer and organizer at the beginning of the nineteenth century. She devoted much of her time and energy to training young girls in the new ways and publicized the fine quality of island tweed amongst her society friends in Edinburgh and London.

The Harris Tweed Association was formed in 1909 when the Globe trademark was officially registered, describing the material in the following terms: 'Harris Tweed means a tweed, hand spun, hand woven, dyed and finished by hand in the islands of Lewis, Harris, Uist, Barra and their several purtenances and all known as the Outer Hebrides.'

The description was redefined in 1934, after great debate and a great deal of ill-feeling: 'Harris Tweed means a tweed made from pure virgin wool, produced in Scotland, spun, dried and finished in the Outer Hebrides and hand woven by the islanders in their own homes in the islands of Lewis, Harris, Uist, Barra and their several purtenances known as the Outer Hebrides.'

This important alteration allowed for the introduction of greater mechanization and an increase in the production of Harris Tweed. However, by the 1960s, many firms outside the Hebrides were producing cloth also marketed as Harris Tweed, although it had never been anywhere near the islands.

In a famous court case in Edinburgh in 1964, lasting sixty-one days, Lord Hunter decided the matter in favour of the Harris Tweed Association. In his 100-page judgement, Lord Hunter referred to the evidence given by James Shaw Grant, who accurately defined the importance of the industry to the islands' economy: 'the Harris Tweed industry must be concerned with the economy of the islands, because it is for that purpose that the tweed came into existence and the name was first publicised.' Had the decision gone against the Association, it is more than likely that the manufacture of Harris Tweed would have eventually become just another victim of increasing centralization: a pawn in the hands of some faceless multi-national organization. Instead, the industry was happily protected from unfair mainland competition and it has prospered and thrived ever since.

OVERLEAF *Seafood galore – lobster pots stacked high on the quay at Cromore*

Guarding the car

My destination that night was Shiltenish, a small village on the south shore of the sea-loch Erisort, on the east coast of Lewis, near Balallan. I turned instinctively left at the roundabout at the end of town. As I ploughed along the wet roads, more 'ship' than car, disconsolate-looking, dripping, black-faced sheep blinked, green-eyed in my headlights.

Crossing Arnish Moor, the moon climbed clear, casting silver spears of light in long shadows across roadside lochans. Bright stars beckoned me southwards and as I passed a cottage, the sharp, acrid smell of peat smoke filled the car. I felt that I had come home, and sang a rousing Gaelic chorus in welcome.

Later that evening, I sat in the bar of the hotel, having a night-cap, surrounded by the musical buzz of Gaelic conversation — long tales and stories. Groups of men, heads confidentially close, listening intently; then loud bursts of delight.

An old man, red-faced and nursing a dram, ambled over and sat down companionably beside me. Within three minutes he had asked my name, where I came from, where I was going, how long I was staying, what I was doing and, since I had a car, the state of my bank balance. Also, for good measure, he inquired, politely, was I married, did I have a family, how many children did I have and if so, where was my wife? I was saved by the entrance of three middle-aged, well-dressed ladies, who burst into the bar in full sail, ordered drams-all-round, and settled in a corner by the fire to chatter with my inquisitive companion. All in Gaelic. I felt like a man from Mars, eavesdropping on a conversation I couldn't understand; but the old charmer had them laughing wildly within seconds.

Lewis is famous for the quality of its game fishing, salmon, sea-trout and brown trout; I once tried to count the freshwater lochs on Lewis and ran out of steam and patience at about 1,600. But I quickly learned that night that local people were not much given to fishing with a rod and line: they prefer more direct methods — such as nets — to catch their fish.

I heard two young men at the bar talking about a recent Sunday fishing expedition: 'Damn it, James, I had hardly got the net out when guess what happened?' one said to the other. 'What happened, Donald?' came the expectant reply. 'Two bloody salmon jumped straight into the boat by themselves!'

Nor does the strict morality of Lewis extend entirely into forbidding poaching activities on the Sabbath — providing that you are not caught. One poacher regularly takes his haul on Saturday night, sells the catch in Stornoway on Sunday morning and then spends much of the proceeds in the pub on his way home on Sunday night.

When I opened the curtains of my bedroom window the following morning, I looked out on a fine, sparkling new day. Sunlight washed the calm, blue and silver waters of Loch Erisort. A gentle breeze ruffled the yellow-brown grass by the shore. Peat smoke drifted lazily from the chimneys of houses across the bay at Balallan.

By breakfast time, however, barely an hour later, it was an entirely different matter; rain was lashing the moorlands in rage and an almighty wind shook the windows. The two kittens I had watched earlier, tumbling in the warm morning, had vanished and the waters of the loch were churned into a frenzy of flying foam. I dashed through the storm to the car. Then dashed back again to collect my camera and maps, which I had forgotten. Whilst I did so, Jekyll and Hyde-like, the weather changed again; rain passed as suddenly as it had arrived and Lewis was all light and laughter once more.

Sudden changes in the weather are part of the Hebridean way of life and islanders are well-accustomed to them. However, for visitors, it can be disconcerting. You quickly learn always to be prepared, however; to keep an eye open, skywards and over the hills, to see what may be coming your way. Clouds gathering in anger over Clisham and Mulla-fo-dheas in Harris almost certainly mean rain is on its way.

North and east Lewis is a tangled, stone-strewn, peat covered landscape, pierced by sea-lochs, fingering deep into bleak moor-

Collecting the 'messages' from the mobile butcher

families stayed.

Their summer shielings were always sited in warm, sunny corners, by good grazing on dry pastures, and sheltered by the slope of a small hill, near fresh water — Arighean Beinn nan Caorach, in Ness; Loch Sleitir by Barvas; the south face of Beinn Bragar; Beinn Choinnich and Beinn Rahacleit, east of Carloway; and many more.

Hundreds of tiny streams blush bright silver after storms, washing over the moors to greet loch and sea. The outlets of many of these streams have been constricted by the building of narrow piers, holding anxious waters back, forming small, deep pools: all the easier to catch returning salmon and sea-trout!

A few wind-lashed rowan trees bravely confronted the breeze as I drove north towards Achmore; decked with poor, shrivelled berries, still waiting for autumn birds. An early buzzard floated by on soundless wings. First Arctic fieldfares pecked hungrily in a sparse stubble field. Drooping black cattle chomped by the shores of Loch Soval as I passed by. Soval is one of the well-known Lewis sporting estates. A white Jaguar car stood by the neatly-trimmed privet hedge in front of the Lodge. A heron was fishing the margins of the loch; slate-grey, sternly erect and concentrating, earning his breakfast the hard way. I called 'good morning'.

Six miles north of Balallan, by the crags of Nisreaval, a minor road leads west to join the main Stornoway/Garynahine road. At the junction I saw my hiking companion from the ferry, waiting for a lift south to Harris. He looked as though he had spent a dry night, in spite of the storm, and I gave a wave and a toot as I drove by.

I also came across my first Lewis bus shelter which looked to all intents and purposes like the tail-fin of a rocket, forever waiting to be capped with a body. These practical shelters, made out of concrete, are divided into four or five sections, roofed over with a flat top. No matter from which direction the wind howls or rain drives, there is always shelter; just a question of edging round into another cubicle.

Looking southwards from Achmore and Lochganvich towards

lands. It is sparkled by a constant delight of freshwater lochs, endlessly changing colour with the whims and fancies of cloud and sun; one minute, sparkling azure blue, the next, dull, leaden grey.

The island is like a huge lump of soggy peat. Agricultural land, other than in the vicinity of Stornoway and the western coastal areas, is sparse and the soils poor. Islanders grow oats, barley, turnip and potatoes and graze cattle and sheep on the moorlands.

In times past, whole communities used to spend the summer months out in the hills, where their cattle found food in plenty after the long confinement of harsh winter months. The map of Lewis is covered with hundreds of these now deserted shielings where

Roineval and Beinn a'Bhoth, the moorlands sparkled with fine lochs: na Gainmhich, na Creige Guirme, Tana and an Daimh. All full of brightly marked, hard fighting wild brown trout. Where even the worst fisherman in the world will catch breakfast, lunch and supper.

I braked for a flock of sheep, ruminating in the middle of the road. Small groups of houses clustered the verges, all seeming to offer Bed and Breakfast accommodation. The visitor to Lewis need never be stuck for somewhere to stay. Everywhere, peat banks blackening the moor; mile after mile of cuttings, lined with stacks of neat, black, winter fuel.

The growth industry of the islands is fish farming, and the income it produces almost rivals that from Harris Tweed. The sad difference is that the fish industry is controlled by multi-national organizations, rather than by the islanders themselves. Upwards of 2,000 people are employed in fish farming in the North of Scotland and Marine Harvest, one of the principal companies, is a major employer of labour in Lewis.

North and south of the road near Garynahine, closely packed lines of lodge-pole pine and Sitka spruce cover the moor; but as yet, forestry is minimal on the Outer Hebrides, compared to the devastation being caused by tree-farmers on mainland Scotland. There, hundreds of thousands of acres have been planted, destroying the view of many wonderful hills, glens and moors.

The 'Heather Isle' has been virtually devoid of trees for almost 1,000 years. Prior to that, much of the island was covered with fine stands of dwarf oak, birch, willow, rowan and pine. The Vikings, displaying their usual lack of regard for anything not 'portable', burned most of the remaining Lewis forests – along with anything else foolish enough to get in their way.

By the white bulk of Garynahine Lodge I swung left and south, following the excellent road to Grimersta, exclusive mecca to generations of salmon fishers, spoken of in whispers and with baited breath: Bridge Pool; Captain's Pool; Long and Battery Pools; magnificent Loch Faoghail an Tuim and Faoghail Charrasan; Faoghail Kirraval and Macley's Stream.

I hung over the bridge, like a child gazing into a sweetshop window, watching in wonder as salmon thrashed and powered their way upstream. Bars of Atlantic-hardened silver, mighty tails, like shining sails, knifing through the tumbling, white and brown, peat-stained waters.

The river is well furnished with man-made pools, steps and weirs, pots and runs, all immaculately maintained and cared for. I also noticed extensive peat cuttings, close to the north bank of the river and imagined a court-room scene: 'Och, to be sure your honour, I was just minding my own business, cutting my peats here, when the beast threw itself straight from the river and landed in the boot of my car, all by itself!'

From Garynahine to just past Grimersta, the B8011 road is excellent; beautifully surfaced and as good as any principal route in Britain, but this excellence is short lived. With a sickening thump, I ran off the smooth, twentieth-century tarmac surface, back onto the narrow, pot-holed, single-track nightmare of times past.

Nevertheless, even these tortuous little roads must have seemed miraculous when they were first built. From 1844 until 1883, 156 miles of roads were constructed, bringing the total mileage of roads on the islands to 200; encouraging physical and mental communication between the remote, isolated townships, particularly those in south and west Lewis and in Harris.

Before these roads were built a journey to the next village was a major expedition, never mind travelling to Stornoway or mainland Scotland. Communities developed separately, each with its own distinct customs, traditions and loyalties. People in these hamlets lived together and relied upon each other very much as a group, rather than as individuals; learning the hard way to look after themselves. In spite of years of disruption, clearances and hardships, that same community spirit is as much alive today as it was in times gone by.

'Take me back to Carloway,' the scattered houses seen from across the inlet

2
LEWIS

UIG, CALLANISH, BARVAS
AND THE BUTT OF LEWIS

Winding over the hill towards Ben Mocacleit and Little Loch Roag, the moorlands southwards seemed to be more water than land; an endless succession of lochs and lochans, sparkling in September sunlight from sweeping, terraced ridges, fading into gold and green mountains, shaped from Lewisian gneiss, the oldest rocks on Earth.

Cattle grids bar the road and as I clattered over yet another, I re-named them 'rattle grids'. I drew into a passing place for an approaching vehicle. A ministered Morris Minor bumped by and I got a cheery wave from the driver, black-suited as his car, white-collared and bustling to Kirk.

On my right lay the ornate entrance to Scaliscro Lodge, a Lewis sporting estate. White pillars topped with slabs painted bright blue. White, firmly shut, wrought-iron gates barred the long drive-way; an incongruous infant 'dog-house' squatted on the left, blue-roofed and white-walled, to shelter milk and mail from rain.

At the head of Little Loch Roag, below the rock-strewn slopes of Caultrashal Beag, the delightful River Morsgail hurries seawards; drawing returning salmon to Morsgail Loch, where a fine Estate Lodge hugs the north-west shore. A notice at the roadside warns passers-by to do just that: PRIVATE ROAD. NO DOGS ALLOWED.

A track leads southwards round Morsgail, out into the wild hills of Morsgail Deer Forest. It is bounded eastwards by Loch Langa-vat, the largest freshwater loch on Lewis and westwards by a long ribbon of streams and lochans that reach the sea at Kinloch-resort.

The remains of some of the oldest houses in Lewis lie by the shores of Kinloch-resort, in the heart of this remote, wilderness land. There are beehive dwellings of prehistoric man, surrounded by the grey walls of ruined summer shielings; but the old voices have gone to be replaced by the angry burr of Argocat and sharp crack of high-powered stalking rifles.

The road becomes ever more tortuous, passing the square bulk of the power station at Gisla on the south shore of Roag. Hardly

enough grass to feed a dormouse, let alone anything else. Granite boulders lurch black-brown from peat hags. Deer grass, bright-green from underground springs, struggles to survive.

A farm by the loch centres the only arable land. Conical, hay-dressed stacks amidst the remains of ancient feannagan taomaidh, lazy-beds; surrounded by small, neat, well-tended, modern, fields. Due to the infertility of soil in the Outer Hebrides, particularly on Lewis and Harris, the islanders devised a system of cultivation which gave them the best opportunity of growing sparse crops on their inhospitable land: they were called lazy-beds. Two trenches were dug, parallel to each other, about ten feet in length and six feet apart. The area between was spread with animal manure or seaweed and then the excavated soil was placed on top. Crops were planted and grown in the middle.

Hundreds of acres of lazy-beds scar the hillsides and the amount of work involved in their construction and maintenance must have represented an enormous investment of time and energy. Nothing could have been less 'lazy' and the crofters relied upon these narrow strips to provide enough food to see them and their stock through the harsh, wind-swept Hebridean winters.

On the hill past Enaclete I stopped and looked towards Ungeshader, where Little Loch Roag is forced into a narrow, seaweed-fringed channel, pointing towards its 'big brother', Loch Roag and the Atlantic Ocean. Dark islets and green islands scatter the blue surface.

The largest island is Great Bernera, joined to the mainland by a causeway over the narrow straits of South Eashader. The people of Great Bernera claim the unique distinction of being one of the few Highland communities to successfully oppose their factor during the dreadful nineteenth-century clearances — when islanders were evicted from their lands and homes to make way for sheep.

The factor concerned was the infamous Donald Munro, known as the 'Shah', hated and despised throughout Lewis and Harris because of his autocratic treatment of the islanders. Under Sir James

The grotto in Stornoway Castle Gardens

Matheson, the tea magnate, who owned the islands, Munro held absolute power over the people and used it ruthlessly. With neither consultation nor compassion, over a period of years, Munro restricted the Bernera crofters' summer-grazing lands; each time, insisting that the crofters build and maintain, at their own expense, dry-stone dykes to keep their stock out of the new sheep farms and deer forests he was creating.

No sooner had the crofters complied with one demand, than further demands and restrictions were made. Reluctance to comply with the factor's instructions were met with the ominous threat of eviction. Ultimately, in 1874, Munro announced that in future, the crofters would have to confine all their stock to Great Bernera. Thus deprived of vital summer-grazing for their animals, the crofters complained. Eviction notices were issued and served, in person, by Munro, along with the Sheriff Officer and a Customs Officer. There was some shouting and throwing of stones, during which Munro claimed that he had been assaulted.

A few days later, a Bernera man was arrested in Stornoway and charged with assault. When news of the arrest reached Bernera, nearly 300 men marched to Stornoway to demand their neighbour's release but Sir James Matheson intervened and the charge was dismissed. Not satisfied with this affront to his dignity, Munro, who held nearly every important official position on Lewis, arranged for three of the principal participants to answer the charge of assault in court and their trial took place in Stornoway in July 1874. They were found not guilty and shortly afterwards Sir James sacked his monstrous factor.

The real pity was Sir James had employed Munro in the first place, and taken such little interest in Munro's activities. Had he done so, then much hardship and suffering, patiently and steadfastly borne, would have been spared the unfortunate inhabitants of his domains.

The road from Enaclete drops northwards by Loch Croistean, marked by one of the few notices printed in English that I saw on

Lewis: PRIVATE FISHING. A trout rose as I passed, dimpling the smooth surface. A small burn with a big name, Abhainn Mhor a'Ghlinne Ruaidh, borders the road; neat with tiny, man-made pools, growing in size towards the sea.

An Historical Heritage Museum invites inspection (except on Sundays) and the road eventually climbs and stumbles down to the sea past the small village of Carishader; then on to Miavaig, busy with road-works and improvements. Tractors Shovels Tawse Limited seem to be doing most of the business and huge chunks of stone, like extracted teeth, have been set on their sides to make an embankment along the shore side of the loch. I stopped at the junction. Which way to Uig? It is not difficult to get lost in Lewis.

A narrow road leads northwards and then divides. I followed the right-hand track and found myself twisting and turning out to Reef; past an amazingly modern, excellent jetty at Uigen. Loch Roag was, and still is, noted for its fishing and stocks of shellfish: lobster, oysters, mussels and whelks. In the early years of the nineteenth century, tens of thousands of lobsters were sent to London markets direct from Loch Roag.

Wide, white sands fringe the dunes at Traigh na Berie on the north coast, looking towards the holy island of Pabay Mor, 'the Priest's Island'; the remains of the tiny church on the island mark a place of worship that was probably in use more than fifteen centuries ago.

Traigh na Berie is a bird sanctuary, and in the hills behind the machair, on two small lochans, there are the remains of a prehistoric dun and a 2,000-year-old broch. A small stream leads from a third lochan, crossing the track towards the north end of the beach, and along its length are the relics of four Norse Grain Mills which were still used until about 1830.

The beach at Traigh na Berie is ideal for a family outing where the bucket and spade brigade may splash and play safely in the clear, blue and green waters of the bay, whilst adults laze away a pleasant hour or two, watching the gentle Hebridean world go by.

Drystone walling at Stornoway Castle

Washed by endless Atlantic Waves — the windswept coastline of Aird Fenish by Mangersta

On the west side of the peninsula, deep within the sheltering arms of Rubha Brataig and Tao Mor is Camas na Clibhe, another magnificent bay, fringed by golden sands. A small, deserted crescent of delight; but be warned, it is not safe for swimming due to strong, dangerous currents. I stopped by Valtos School Adventure Centre overlooking the bay, and had lunch, wondering at the peace, solitude and beauty of the view.

Suddenly, from left to right, panting along the sands, came the figure of a lone man, naked except for shorts, jogging heavily across the beach. Keeping fit; but I couldn't help wondering what the Free Church would have to say about his state of undress and 'un-Christian' Sabbath activity. The man lumbered up to the cemetery, paused to catch his breath, then disappeared towards Valtos.

Back at the junction by Dr Hay's surgery and bungalow, I turned down Glen Valtos to Timisgarry and Uig. The glen is being torn apart by road-works. Quarries carved out of the hillside to make foundations for the new road. A few trees cling stubbornly to the hills which are almost completely bare of vegetation. Scraps of heather nestle bravely by granite rocks.

I discovered Uig more years ago than I care to remember. Not by visiting, but by being given a replica of a chess set: the Lewis Chessmen. The originals were discovered in 1831, when a cow dislodged them from the sand dunes near Ardroil. The beautiful figures were carved from walrus ivory and probably date from the middle of the twelfth century. Eleven of the seventy-eight tomb-like pieces are preserved in the Scottish National Museum of Antiquities in Edinburgh; the remainder are housed in the British Museum, London. My excellent friends, made under licence in the late 1960s, are regularly dragged out to fight again and again – but, unlike their Viking ancestors, I rarely win.

Uig Lodge dominates the bay; standing like a big, sore white thumb, on a green knowe above Dun Borranish. The house was built as a hunting lodge by Sir James Matheson more than one hundred years ago, and when Lord Leverhulme bought Lewis and

Harris from Sir James, he presented the lodge to his niece, Emily MacDonald, as a wedding present. As her diary reveals, Emily was entranced:

> We gazed upon a scene which surely has few equals in all Britain for sheer, breathtaking loveliness. On the left in awe-inspiring grandeur stood a semicircle of grey rugged mountains. Below, cool blue lochs lay shimmering in the sunlight.
>
> The Lodge, a white house surmounted by a tower, stands on a flower-decked grassy eminence above the most beautiful bay it has ever been my privilege to see; indeed, I could imagine no scene of greater beauty than that which lay before us. Miles of sheer white sand extended far out into the west, where it rippled the tide as it flowed from the Atlantic Ocean.
>
> A river wound its way from the lochs and half-circled the bay 'ere it reached the sea. Green headlands stretched craggy arms of black rock to left and right at the outlet of the bay, guarding this gem of beauty from the full fury of the Atlantic storms.
>
> But what I found so overwhelmingly impressive was the spiritual quality of the place, which extended even to the Lodge itself. It was something I had never before felt or seen — a timelessness and healing peace, a dreaming beauty over all which seemed not of this earth.

The 'spiritual quality' so much admired by Emily MacDonald, is cared for today by the Rev. W. Macleod, who looks after Uig and Timsgarry parish. Timsgarry church bell is tolled from the outside of the building, a rope dangling down the wall, and the church gazes southwards across shining white sands towards the corries and peaks of Mealisval and Tahaval.

Close by is the local school, ultra-modern and incongruous. As I watched the endless waves, rolling in from their long Atlantic journey, the weather changed and it started to rain again. Uig Lodge disappeared in a grey mist. The old house is used today, as it was

when Sir James Matheson built it, as a sporting lodge — exclusive and expensive.

I turned from the view and drove northwards, back up gaunt Glen Valtos, pondering upon the inequalities of life. In the days of Matheson, Leverhulme and MacDonald, the stags on the hill and fish in the rivers were not for Lewismen nor their families. Nor are they today.

I wondered how much time the old islanders had to spare from the unending toil of their existence, to consider the 'spiritual quality . . . healing peace . . . dreaming beauty' of their island? How much their lairds really cared for, or understood, the people whom they 'owned'?

As I drove north, silver streams cascaded down Glen Valtos from Ben Miavaig and Forsnaval, gathering together in a tiny river, gurgling and splashing seawards to Loch Roag. As you drive down the glen, look carefully at either side; the gorge was formed, a millennium ago, by a violent earth tremor. Each split and crack on one side has an equal and opposite split and crack on the other.

Suddenly, my first Lewis traffic jam, in Glen Valtos. Three other cars returning from church at Miavaig. Two churches at Miavaig: Uig Parish Church and the Free Presbytery Church. A long stream of cars now, all blessed and homeward bound.

As I wound carefully along the narrow loch-side road, four red hens squawked angrily in front of the car, feathers wrongly ruffled by the sharp west wind. A single heron fished, statuesque, by the shore. Waiting for his Sunday offering. The air was full of the scent of peat fires, poked to life after morning service. Black, plastic rubbish bins, waiting for collection, marked the ends of farm tracks: NO HOT ASHES.

Much of the road had been scraped bare in readiness for a new, pristine tarmac surface and I bumped and bucketed over bare rock. Small, white posts by the side of the road mark the extent of personal peat-patches; and some of the lazy-beds still seem to be worked for there were piles of green seaweed lying by them, waiting to be spread.

I drove by Gisla and Morsgail and climbed the hill past Loch an Eilein; eastwards, waves on lochs Mehal Beag and Fhir Mhaoil were combed and crested grey and white by the wind. At the top of the hill I looked towards Garynahine and Orasay island. Beyond them, perched on a bare, green hillside, half-circled by water, rose the magnificent Callanish Standing Stones: a sudden series of dark apostrophes against the bright sky.

Turning onto the main road I fell in behind a minibus, obviously heading for Callanish as well, and we lurched in convoy through yet more road-works, then onto a superbly surfaced section of new road. A mile later we turned left and low-geared and laboured up the narrow, twisting track which leads to the old grey stones, cresting a sparse plateau, 100 feet above the sea.

The Callanish Standing Stones are one of the most dramatic and important Neolithic monuments in Europe, probably erected some 4,500 years ago and certainly as significant as Stonehenge. They were first excavated in 1856 on the instructions of Sir James Matheson, when more than five feet of peat had to be removed to fully expose them. Forty-eight sculptured slabs remain, finely textured, almost surreal, dominated by a mighty central pillar 15 feet 7 inches high and one foot thick. The ruins of a chambered burial cairn lie at the foot of the great centre stone, guarded by its sombre, sentinel companions.

Callanish Farm, close to the stones and extending to 200 acres, was bought by Edinburgh University Archaeology Department in 1985 as a study area, in order to research prehistoric remains and the life and work of early settlers of the heather isles.

The west coast of Lewis, from Uig northwards, has a rich variety of ancient monuments: standing stones, chambered cairns, crannogs, duns and brochs. Evidence of a widely settled land, inhabited by an established, cultured society. What secrets lie waiting to be discovered, beneath the sands, grassy mounds and shallow waters of the lochs?

A local society, Cearcall Chalanais, Friends of Callanish, are

The dramatic ruins of Carloway Broch, one of the most complete examples of these ancient fortified houses

OVERLEAF *An unending vista of moorland and water — the hinterland of Pairc taken from the hills above Orinsay*

helping to discover them and Professor Dennis Harding, Edinburgh University's research director, explained recently in the *Scotsman* newspaper the progress being made and why the site was of such great importance:

> In the Western Isles we have evidence of a strongly integrated society from Neolithic through Iron Age times. It was not a humble, a 'squalor' economy, but one that thrived on the fertile coastal plains and we have every reason to suppose had contacts, possibly trading ones, by sea with mainland Scotland and other parts.
>
> The whole network of sites on the west coast of Lewis suggests a major focus. The Callanish Stones themselves show this. It doesn't matter about the character of the ritual that placed them there: they represent a formally structured society.

There are plans for a visitor centre at Callanish Farm and also to construct a replica of an Iron Age wheelhouse. Cearcall Chalanais' secretary, Norma Mackenzie explains the proposals in their brochure seeking public support for this project:

> Experiments in prehistoric building techniques are planned, and it is hoped to build 'new' wheelhouses and other structures – possibly souterrains and even galleried duns (brochs) – in the hope of answering questions about their construction, roofing and stability.
>
> This would develop as an Archaeological Theme Park at Callanish Farm (out of sight of the Callanish Stones), which would be open to the public, who would be able to visit the cultivated fields and livestock areas. Demonstrations of potting and smelting may also be available during summer.

The farm is to be worked, as far as possible, using the same crop as ancient man, planting foureared barley. It is part of a twentyfiveyear research programme designed to investigate the field systems and agricultural methods used by Neolithic man at Callanish in order to establish a 'permanent academic presence' and fulfil 'an important educational function'.

As I followed the road northwards past Breasclete the landscape grew wilder, rougher; rock-strewn hills crowding the way, a minia-ture Highlands, enclosing more than thirty freshwater lochs between the sea and the Pentland Road. This old track, twenty miles in length from Carloway to Stornoway, was built in 1882 to provide work for the islanders who were facing famine yet again after fierce weather had destroyed many of their crops.

A brightly painted lighthouse crowns a rocky outcrop in East Loch Roag; nearby, a fish processing plant and fish farm seem strangely out of place in such desolate surroundings. By the ridge of Buailaval Mor and scattered hamlet of Doune Carloway, I parked and climbed the wet track to the Pictish Broch on the hill; one of the best preserved examples of a broch in the north. These massive, dry-stone structures were built between 200 BC and AD 200. How-ever, the enigma of the brochs is that no one knows why such huge defensive homes were required. The Romans never seriously attempted to invade the far north; marauding Vikings didn't arrive on the scene until after the brochs were built. Who was the enemy?

My own theory is that over the years, times have little changed, I have this irreverent vision of a worried prehistoric man, peering from his tower, watching the approach of some mother-in-law, or other unwelcome relations, yelling down, telling his family to: 'Bar the gate! Keep quiet and pretend we are out. Perhaps they'll go away!'

Carloway broch crowns a grassy hillock, looking south over Loch an Duin, and north across fertile fields to Loch Carloway. Part of the circular walls of the broch are still 30 feet high and they enclose a courtyard 25 feet in diameter. They were built with a double wall, approximately 10 feet thick, enclosing a stairway to the top. They were open to the elements and had no windows on the outside walls. The entrance was a narrow passage and at Carloway this entrance is well preserved and still provides access today. Sadly,

The crenellated silhouette of Lews Castle College, Stornoway, which dominates the harbour

over the years, much of the broch has been dismantled by 'stone robbers', but it is now preserved and cared for by the Historical Monuments Society.

Carloway broch is a dramatic ruin and a fine example of these ancient fortifications. It also has a more modern history, because the brochs were used for many centuries after their original occupants had been either, murdered, banished or 'integrated' with more powerful invaders.

In the seventeenth century, Donald Cam MacAulay from Uig managed to trap a number of his enemies, the MacKays from Ross-shire, in Carloway broch: they, secure inside; Donald, furious with-out. Using two dirks as alternate hand- and foot-holds, Donald scaled the walls – and fell upon his foes.

I fell upon Carloway just as church was coming out. More than 100 cars were lined up outside the gaunt, rectangular, forbidding looking building. Sombrely-attired islanders flooded from the church and the village was suddenly more busy than any other place I had visited in the north.

A bevy of black crows circled over something dead in a field and the skies opened and rain poured down, sending the congregation scurrying towards the shelter of their vehicles. I switched on head-lights, although it was barely half past one, and drove cautiously, following the long line of cars. One by one they turned, left and right to their homes, until I was alone once more.

A cluster of Shawbosts appeared through the gloom: South Shawbost, Shawbost, New Shawbost and North Shawbost. Just before the village, at the end of Loch Raoinavat (the Rowan Loch), a gate in the fence leads round the north shore to another Lewis ancient monument, the Shawbost Stone Circle.

This site, like Carloway, has been much robbed of its stones over the years but Margaret and Rebecca Ponting, and Mysie Macrae have produced an excellent guide to the remaining features. It is thought that perhaps twelve stones formed the ring but after the First World War some were spirited away and built into surrounding dwellings. The guide also describes a land dispute that took place about 100 years ago between the people of Dalbeg and Shawbost regarding village boundaries:

> The people from Dalbeg built a turf wall furthest east, giving themselves more land. One night, the Shawbost people knocked it down; a dry stone wall was built and is once more the boundary between Dalbeg and Shawbost.

> The turf wall has the Gaelic name of Sean Gharaidh, meaning 'the old wall'. The dry stone wall is called an Garadh Geal in Gaelic, 'the white wall'. The island with the cairn [in the loch], Eilean an Tighe means 'the island of the house'. Ashes and other remains were found there by Norman Morrison of Shawbost earlier this century.

A very wet mallard scuttled into rushes fringeing the shore of one more Loch an Duna as I approached Bragar. A vast pile of stones, set upon a little promontory marks the site of the broch. The main wall stands to a height of 14 feet and measures up to 12 foot thick, enclosing an area of 30 feet. Details of most of the ancient monu-ments in Scotland can be found in Richard Feacham's excellent publication, *Guide to Prehistoric Scotland*; but so little work has been done on the Hebridean monuments that they alone are worthy of a book to themselves.

North from Shawbost, the jaw-bone of a whale has been made into a vast arch over the entrance to a house by the side of the road at Bragar. The poor beast was stranded on the beach at Port Arnot, north of the village, and after being killed and flenched, the jaw-bone was used as decoration. The harpoon spear that delivered the fatal blow is transfixed to the top of the jaw, like a frightening sword of Damocles.

One of the most dramatic of the Lewis Neolithic monuments is Clach an Trushal: a giant, single, standing stone near Ballantrushal. The stone is 19 foot high, 6 foot wide and 3 foot, 9 inches thick, tapering to a width of one foot at the top. The old story is that Clach

Bagging up sand at Lemieway

In dry dock at Barvas

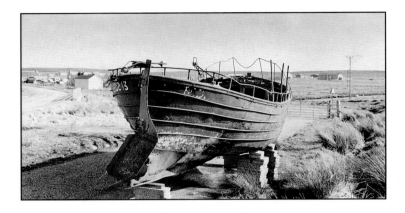

an Trushal is really a petrified man, turned into stone for some dreadful, long-forgotten misdemeanour.

As I passed Five Penny Borve, the rain stopped and the sun slid out from behind threatening clouds. This quaint name commemorates the system used to measure land up until the end of the eighteenth century, when new-fangled 'acres' were introduced. The principal units were davachs and pennylands, based upon the numbers of beasts the land could support. One davach consisted of twenty pennylands. Hundreds of thousands of davachs stretch eastwards across the Parish of Ness to the Minch, but they were little used in times past, other than for summer grazings. These wild, empty moorlands are devoid of roads and have few tracks. The only way in is by Shanks's pony.

And hard walking country it is. But what a delight when you get there. Rich in bird life and wild flowers, scattered with dozens of trout-filled lochs; a wilderness landscape where you may walk for days without meeting another soul. The stuff that dreams are made of, perfect solitude.

A cluster of small villages announces the end of the road: Cross, Swainbost, Habost and Lionel. From here a minor road triangles the northern tip of the island. The two arms are given different, profligate numberings: B8013 south and B8014 north. Neither are more than a couple of miles in length and they meet at the township of Eoropie.

In a field to the north of the village stands the carefully restored church of Eoropie Teampull, St Molua's Church, the property of the Episcopal Church of Scotland, cared for by the priest of St Peter's Episcopal Church, Stornoway. St Molua's was probably built during the twelfth century but much of the evidence required to verify dating vanished when restoration works were carried out in 1912. Nevertheless, it is possible that the site was used for Celtic and Christian religious ceremonies, and, surprisingly, often for both at the same time.

Local historian, Gerald Ponting, in his notes on Eoropie Teampull, explains:

> In the early Celtic Church many of the Christian saints were actually adopted pagan Celtic gods and goddesses. The 'lua' syllable of Molua may have been derived from the sea-god Lug, so the life-story of Molua, who supposedly died in AD 592 may be pure invention.

Towards the end of the seventeenth century, Martin Martin, tutor to the children of Macleod of Dunvegan, visited Lewis and described an annual pagan celebration which he reported had still been practised at St Molua in the 1660s. Gerald Ponting records:

> Martin's account stated that families from around the island brought malt with them and brewed ale. A man waded into the sea at night, up to his waist, held a cup of ale aloft and cried: 'Shony, I give you this cup of ale, hoping that you'll be so kind as to send up plenty of sea-ware for enriching our ground the ensuing year.' He then threw the cup of ale into the sea.

> Then everyone went to the church, where, according to Martin Martin: 'there was a Candle burning upon the Altar; and then standing silent for a little time, one of them gave a

signal, at which the Candle was put out, and immediately all of them went into the fields, where they fell a drinking their Ale and spent the remainder of the Night in Dancing and Singing etc.'

One cannot help but regret that the otherwise erudite and observant Mr Martin failed to delineate exactly what the 'etc.' included. I would love to know. But it seems a strange quirk of fate that this site would have proved to be such an enduring religious focal point for such differing faiths: Celtic and Christian. It is equally strange that this small Episcopal enclave should survive, surrounded as it is by such Calvanistic fervour.

A fair amount of dancing and drinking still takes place in the Parish of Ness and the Ness Football Club have it all extremely well organized. In front of their immaculate clubhouse, the well-tended turf is surrounded by green and white painted railings, attached to which are advertising placards for local businesses. Conveniently adjacent to the football field is the Ness Social Club – for pre-football cheer. I'm sure St Molua would have approved – and probably the Viking sea-god Lug, too.

A track leads from Eoropie down to the shore, where white sand dunes mingle with green fields. The coast southwards is indented with several beaches: Traigh Sands, Swainbost Sands, Traigh Chumil and Cross Sands. The comfortable Ness Inn provides an ideal centre for exploring this magnificent coastline.

Northwards, past Teampull Mholuaidh, a narrow road leads out to land's end at the Butt of Lewis. A huge pattern of lazy-beds borders the road. Jagged, black cliffs fall to enclose a perfect, sheltered, sandy beach on the east of the peninsula at Port Sto. Then the shock of the lighthouse constructed out of red brick, contrasting vividly with the white and brown of the keeper's house and out-buildings.

I walked to the edge of the cliffs. Forty miles distant, north-east, across the storm-tossed waves lay the tiny island of North Rona, uninhabited since 1884 when the last two settlers, the Mackays from

Ness, perished, alone, from illness and exposure.

South-west from Rona, lies the rocky eminence of Sulisgeir, still visited today each September by the men of Ness to hunt for gannets. They inch past Thamna Sgeir to Geodha a'Phuill Bhain, where there is an iron ring in the rocks for securing the boat, before scrambling ashore to catch the young birds just before they learn to fly.

Next stop Iceland. A fulmar swept by on stiff, motionless wings. Seagulls danced above the waves. The ocean sang as if in rage, beating its heart and soul against the stacks and cliffs of Lewis. I felt like a speck of dust amidst the timeless universe. Insignificant, vulnerable, transient.

I thought of the islanders and their struggles throughout the ages. With Vikings, Lowland Scots, lairds and English landlords, living out their harsh, demanding lives amidst these wild, unforgiving lands. Determined, in spite of everything, to survive. Donald Macdonald, in his book *Lewis: A History of the Island*, sums it up: 'Is treise Tuath na Tighearna' – Tenantry are stronger than the Laird.

3
HARRIS

I celebrated my fiftieth birthday in Balallan on Lewis. In the morning, I immediately checked over various bits of the Royal Personage, to ensure that nothing had dropped off during the night. Tried a tentative song. Recited a few lines of poetry. Remembered something really difficult; but in spite of my worst fears, everything appeared to be in working order. So welcome the half-century! Not so bad as people make out.

A dreich, damp day greeted me, full of mist and rain. I packed my bags, paid my account and headed for the book-mobile; the name given by my family to the old cars I buy to use whilst researching books. This particular model, an ancient Mini Clubman had served me well and started, as always, with the first turn of the key.

A storm the previous night had turned even the smallest streams into raging torrents and hills were streaked white with urgent waters rushing to the sea. South of Balallan, I stopped by the triangle of Loch Chipain, to the right of the road below the slopes of Beinn a'Mhuil, where the route is forced to the edge of Loch Seaforth. The sun broke through and the clouds lifted, giving me a first glimpse of glorious Harris.

Aline Lodge, with its cluster of cottages and tiny jetty, crouched by the shore; peat smoke wisping lazily upwards in the calm morning breeze. A rough track contoured westwards through a narrow glen, leading to the ragged seven-mile length of Loch Langavat, famous for salmon and trout fishing; along the wet line of the old dyke, where Abhainn a' Mhuil hurries seawards from the summer shielings at Creag na Clibhe.

Loch Seaforth lay before me, a ribbon of sparkling silver, dominated by the steep, dark cliffs of Seaforth Island, guarding the head of the loch. Range after range of sombre mountains, Muaithabhal, Beinn Mhor, Carn Ban and Caiteshal, marched eastwards across the Parish of Pairc, through Eishken to the Minch.

A single road pierces this moorland solitude, winding over the hill from near Balallan to greet the eastern arm of Loch Seaforth by Seaforth Head and Loch Sgibacleit, following the right shore, and

A waterfall at Amhuinnsuidhe, where salmon run

then plunging south to Eishken Lodge with its surprising, beautifully-wooded gardens overlooking the narrow inlet of Tob Eishken on the margins of Loch Sealg.

The remainder of Eishken is a trackless wilderness, knifed by the jagged sea-scars of Lochs Sealg and Odhairn, scattered with countless lochs and lochans, burns and streams, secret glens and dark corries. Home of red deer, golden eagle and mountain hare; bounded on the east by the tortuous road from Garyvard to the little village of Lemreway at Rubha Gholl Shuil, protected by Eilean Iubhard in Caolas a'Tuath bay.

Southwards, ringed by the sharp rocks of Sgurr Scaladale, Aonaig Mhor and Mulla-fo-dheas, rears Clisham, the highest mountain in the Outer Hebrides, cloud-capped and beckoning. Compass and map, climbing country, challenging and demanding. This is where a sudden mist or storm can sweep in disorientating even the most experienced mountaineer. A land where caution is the watch-word.

Caution has always been an important island watch-word, given the Hebrides' turbulent history and the precarious nature of life. In 1266, soon after King Alexander III had broken Viking dominance of the Western Isles at the Battle of Largs, the islands were ceded to Scotland by the Treaty of Perth. But the Norwegian legacy remains, noted in the names of geographical features – and in the features of some of the people, particularly in the Parish of Ness in north Lewis, where to this day there are uncharacteristically blue-eyed, fair-haired, tall islanders.

However, the people of Harris have retained a more Celtic appearance; greatly protected from Viking and other influences by the outlandish nature of their wild land. Surrounded by mountains, with villages and townships widely separated by miles of difficult, dangerous, tortuous tracks, invasion is difficult.

More characteristically, the early history of the 'long isle' was one of almost continual warfare as succeeding lairds fought and squabbled over ownership; the all too frequent, sad Highland story of treason, robbery, murder, revenge and extortion.

When clan fought clan, brother fought brother and fathers sometimes arranged for the 'permanent' removal of unruly offspring. It has been said of Clan Macleod, the traditional lairds: 'They are like pikes in water. The oldest of them, if the larger, eats the younger.'

Macleods dominated the islands until King James VI of Scotland gained possession by an Act of Parliament in 1579 which required lairds to prove ownership of their land – by producing their title deeds. The Macleods failed to do so and thereby forfeited their lands to the Crown. James then leased the islands to the Fife Adventurers, and sent them northwards, full of hope, in order to pacify the natives, exploit and develop the rich Hebridean fishery and also, hopefully, to replenish his dangerously depleted Royal piggy-bank.

In 1610 the Fife Adventurers admitted defeat by which time King James had abandoned Scotland for London. They sold Lewis to the Mackenzies of Kintail and retired hurt. The Mackenzies (motto 'Helpers of the King') took possession of their new domains and awarded themselves the title of Earls of Seaforth. Great sportsmen, their favourite hunting grounds were in the lands surrounding the deep waters of the loch. The Dunvegan Macleods of Skye maintained a hold on Harris until 1779, but it too eventually fell to the rapacious Mackenzies of Kintail.

However, owning the 'long island' was never easy; and neither the land nor its people were ever rich enough to satisfy the demands of their lairds. Recurring crop failure and famine soon seriously depleted Mackenzie fortunes. Even the glory years of the kelp industry failed to keep pace with the Earls' financial ambitions and eventually, in 1833, the running of the straitened estates was placed in the hands of Trustees.

The end came in 1844; all the old Mackenzie links with Lewis and Harris were finally broken when the widow of Stewart Mackenzie sold the 'long island' to a native of Sutherland, Sir James Matheson.

As I drove past Seaforth Island and began the steep climb up the

north shoulder of Caisteal Ard to Cleet Ard, Harris gave me a proper welcome. The wind rose and a white mist enfolded the hills. Skies opened, pouring down impenetrable sheets of rain. I believe that there is no rain quite like Hebridean rain. At times, it can be so torrential that it is almost impossible to see a hand in front of your face.

Clisham disappeared in disgust as I peered through the windscreen, following the winding, twisting road forever upwards, into the very heart of North Harris. Furious winds swept round encircling hills, as things possessed. Often, within one view, it was possible to see several different types of weather: bright sunlight blinking westwards over the Island of Taransay whilst An Coileach on South Harris lies gripped in a mighty, swirling storm.

This road is one of the most dramatic I have ever travelled. Peaks crowd in on either side, yet the glen is wide enough to give a sense of light and space. The hillsides are alive with streamlets, cascading over broken, granite rocks, plunging down to Loch Seaforth.

I nod a silent prayer, glad that I hadn't been caught out in mountains on such a day. The previous night, the Head Keeper of North Eishken Estate had warned me of the folly of doing so: 'After ten years walking the ground, even in good weather, I can still find myself lost, or up to my neck in some unexpected peat bog.'

Near the top of the glen, between Sorn Carsaclett and Bac a'Ghaill, I braked hard. Through the rain, four figures appeared, attired for climbing, making towards Ardvourlie. They were absolutely drenched; and yet, they lined the road, dripping and waved happily as I splashed past south towards Tarbert.

Inevitable road-works littered the way. I paused to let an unexpected, speeding red Porsche flash by. Loch na Ciste and Loch a Mhorgain lay below, leaden grey, on a peat-black plateau to my left,

Tarbert town and harbour. The Gulf Stream normally keeps the snow away from the Hebrides

rippled by tiny wavelets. A damp buzzard floated serenely overhead on wide wings. Lunch time. Then sun shone brightly once more, drawing a fine haze of steam from the warm tarmac.

At the bottom of the hill, a signpost points the way westwards to Hushinish and the Island of Scarp; a switch-back road, leading out to a famous Harris sporting estate, Amhuinnsuidhe, which covers almost all of North Harris. The road winds past the front of Amhuinnsuidhe Lodge; and along the way notices warn casual visitors to beware of walking in the hills during the stalking season — or risk the danger of being shot. The estate rents out shooting and fishing for upwards of £8,000 per week and sportsmen from all over the world queue to enjoy Amhuinnsuidhe's pleasures.

A few years ago, the owner of the estate tried to force crofters to remove their sheep from his hills, in order to preserve sparse grass for deer. The Crofters' Union and the Nature Conservancy Council intervened, claiming that the notice given to the crofters was too short. The crofters themselves, simply refused to budge; in similar circumstances, their grandfathers and ancestors, in the nineteenth century, had submitted humbly and left. Eventually, the estate gave in and withdrew their demands. Times change.

I drove back to the main road, past the tall, brick-built chimney at Bunavoneadar, once a whaling centre; and where the outlet stream from Loch Sgeireagan Mor dances over the beach into Loch Bun Abhainn-eadar, I turned right to Tarbert.

As I sped round the craggy shoulder of Gillaval Glas, an old, blackened ferry terminal poked an inquisitive, dark finger into West Loch Tarbert; then, suddenly, sunlight glinted on the wet rooftops of the town.

Tarbert is the commercial centre of Harris and the Caledonian McBrayne ferry terminal; a cluster of houses on the narrow neck of land that pinches Harris, like a Victorian widow's hour-glass waist, to a breadth of less than one mile. Well provided with shops, garage, banks and a comfortable, welcoming hotel. A mobile dental clinic sat parked by the grey walls of the school. Teeth time for Tarbert

'Tomcat', a regular at the Rodel Hotel Bar on the southern tip of Harris

children. But even today, with a reasonably efficient road system, going to the dentist or shopping in Harris is a major expedition. The narrow roads leading from the scattered coastal villages are all single-tracked and demanding. On Harris, you get nowhere fast.

In times past, communications must have been very difficult and often a great hardship. The rough tracks over the moors were used by everyone: children plodding the long miles to school, mothers carrying family supplies, fathers taking stock to market. A network of these old routes spider-web from Tarbert. They spread northwards, from Urgha Beag, following the long estuary of Loch Laxadale, the Vikings 'salmon loch', by the west shore of the loch, up the glen, ten miles north to Scaladale. Zig-zagging eastwards, past Carragraich, Ceann a'Gharaidh, Steinish and Kyle Scalpay to Carnach. North-east, by Beinn Tharsuinn and Trollamul to the old shielings at Molinginish; with a further arm leading round the rocky coast to Gary-aloteger and Rhenigidale, where there is one of Scotland's most remote and attractive youth hostels.

The main road south, the only road, climbs from town past Loch Diraclett which is managed and preserved by the Harris Angling Club: Members Only. Strictly Fly Fishing. Good thing too. With all the trout fishing available in the Western Isles, there should be no need for anything other than fly fishing.

I passed the 'Golden Road'. A scrap of metalled-surface, twisting round the fjord-like, east coastline. Decided to come back that way. Horsacleit Lodge, a small sporting estate, lay on my right; a substantial white house, overlooking a tiny loch. At the outfall, a concrete weir has been built, to hold back precious waters in order to create artificial spates.

The small river surges under the road and then plunges down the hill in a series of spectacular waterfalls and pools, gathering briefly in Loch na Larach Leithe before crossing the Golden Road to reach the sea in Loch Ceann Dibig near Meavag. Good sport here with salmon, sea-trout and brown trout, and the owner, Mr Lucas, sometimes lets the lodge and fishing to visitors.

The road twists and climbs into an amazing range of wild hills passing between the twin peaks of Uavla Beg and Groas Cleit. A glorious double rainbow arched westwards across Glen Laxdale. Stunningly beautiful. Several more followed, appearing and fading as light and weather changed with amazing speed.

Small, black peat banks scarred the moor. A few, sparse purple patches of heather still flourished bravely, as though determined to keep winter at bay. The rain poured now, and the rainbows vanished in the storm. The Laxdale River bordered the road; a sheer delight of infant water, growing visibly as it neared the sea. Deep pots, weirs and tumbling runs were banked by heather and yellow deer grass.

At Holm Beg, a minor road points westwards to the village of Luskentyre, with its ancient graveyard overlooking the sands and Sound of Taransay. Along the line of the old Glen Laxdale road, which is to the south of the new road, on the other bank of Laxdale River, stone cairns used to line the way; they marked the places where coffins were rested on their final journey to the cemetery by the shore.

In Lewis, there were no such rests for mourners, on that ultimate journey, awaiting us all. James Shaw Grant, in his book *Surprise Island*, describes the procedure:

> After the service at the house, the coffin is taken out and laid on a bier which rests on four dining room chairs. The nearest male relative takes his place behind the coffin, at the head that is, as it is carried feet foremost. He also takes in his hand one of the cords with which the coffin will eventually be lowered into the grave.
>
> When the coffin has been placed on the bier, the crowd replace their hats, and move silently forward, in pairs, to form a double file on each side of the coffin, with the rest two by two behind. The two inner files lift the bier, four on each side. The chairs are removed, and the slow procession begins.
>
> After twenty paces or so, the leading pair in the outside file exchange a glance, and move in simultaneously to relieve the two who are carrying the forward shafts of the bier. The two who are relieved take over from the two behind them as the bier moves forward, and so on until the fourth, and last, pair in the inner file are relieved completely. They drop out of the procession, one on each side, standing half turned away until the whole procession has passed, whereupon they join it again at the tail.
>
> The whole operation is carried out without direction from anyone, and without halting the procession — a long established local tradition running smoothly under its own momentum of an enduring folk memory. It is possible for a small company to carry a coffin for a considerable distance in this way, without fatigue, which is probably why the processional order was so arranged in the first place.

There is a delightful caravan site at Luskentyre and the hills behind provide some splendid walks, but the most dramatic aspects of the view are the wide, golden sands, fringeing the bay. Harris beaches are outstandingly lovely and some of the finest are to be found along the machair lands of the south-west coast.

The uninhabited island of Taransay guards the mouth of the bay, providing shelter from storms; breaking the long swell of 3,000-mile old waves, sweeping in from the Atlantic. The waters of the bay take on myriad colours which are almost unbelievable: breathtakingly vivid blue, emerald and white. A causeway hurries the road across the shallows, enclosing a small loch, bobbing with fishing boats.

Black and white bibbed oystercatchers were busy working the sands, red bills probing eagerly for food. Early winter redwings thronged the fields, pecking and arguing amongst the stubble. Harris is an ornithologists' dreamland where visiting and resident species are a constant source of delight. Golden eagles nest in the high mountains and are often seen, swooping in lordly grandeur above their vast domains.

OVERLEAF *Glorious Hushinish Beach, unusually free of cattle and hens*

More recently, the magnificent white-tailed eagle has become a regular visitor — and, who knows, it may even establish itself on Harris. These huge birds became extinct during the early years of the twentieth century but the Norwegian species was recently re-introduced to the Island of Rhum by the Nature Conservancy Council, greatly assisted by the Royal Air Force. They have bred successfully and now wheel far out over the turbulent waters of the Minch to visit neighbouring islands.

Other raptors ply the moors and hills: buzzard, peregrine, kestrel, marsh harrier and merlin. An immature golden eagle was very lucky recently. The young bird had been mobbed and attacked by angry fulmars, causing it serious damage. Fortunately, the eagle was found at Tiumpan Head and nursed back to health by the factor of the Garynahine Estate, Andrew Miller Mundy, and his wife, before being released back into the wild.

Sand dunes edge the machair at Horgabost, and the grass is lazy with sombre-eyed, grazing, black-faced sheep. Down on the foreshore is a football pitch, complete with goal posts. Football seems to have a huge following throughout the islands for there are pitches everywhere.

One of the most dramatic Neolithic monuments in South Harris lies to the north of the village; the great Clett Nisabost standing stone, dominating a craggy peninsula overlooking the sea. The Nisabost stone measures 10 feet 6 inches in height, 4 feet 6 inches wide and 1 foot 4 inches thick. Smaller stones are scattered round; two on the west side, placed at right angles to the main slab, and others in between.

I strolled round Clett Nisabost to Borve village, the old South Harris home of Lord Leverhulme; Leverhulme was certainly never stuck for a bed for the night on the heather isles: he owned most of them! Borve Lodge in the village has always been famous for its walled garden and, as I passed a considerable amount of gardening work was still in progress.

Grow-bags protected newly-planted trees from harsh sea-breezes.

Outside Heather Graham's craft centre and workshop at the lodge, Mr Graham was busy giving his lawn its last cut of the season. The contrast between the rugged, rock-scattered hills and gentle machair lands is astonishing. On the one hand, hardly enough soil to grow a sprig; on the other, immediately adjacent, rich, fertile fields, offering the hope of relatively easy living.

In the hills above Borve, by Loch an Duin, are the remains of an ancient broch, and at the side of the road, between Borve and Scarista, is a small, Neolithic standing stone. It is insignificant and easy to miss. Indeed, given that there is neither sign nor notice, I'm surprised it has stood unmolested for so long.

The most exciting prehistoric remains on Harris were discovered in 1964 by Professor James McEwen of Aberdeen University, on Toe Head, amidst the golden sand dunes by Northton: a complete village, occupied for centuries by successive groups, each leaving evidence of their passing from Neolithic times down to the age of the Beaker people. Much has been recovered, including pottery, tools, two small combs, and, in an oval grave, the body of a child.

Other, less serious, excavations regularly take place across the links at Northton where there is an excellent little golf course. However, as you are severely admonished by a notice, playing golf on Sunday is strictly forbidden. And just to make sure that you know, two signs have been erected: on at the south end of the course, the other at the north.

I wonder what would happen if one were discovered Sunday golfing? Or Sunday sun-bathing, naturally, in God's skin, on a remote beach?

Over the hill from Northton now, through Glen Coisheltter, and down into Leverburgh by the sheltered estuary of the Obbe. In the old days, the village by the shore was called Obbe, but it was renamed Leverburgh in 1923, after Lord Leverhulme, who bought Lewis and Harris in 1917.

Leverhulme, known on the islands as 'Bodach an t-siabuinn', the Old Man of the Soap, because of his detergent empire at Port

Scenes from Tarbert High Street, the Harris Tweed Emporium and a Christian bookshop

Sunlight in Cheshire, in his efforts to bring prosperity to the Hebrides, transferred his attention to Harris because of opposition to his plans to stop subsistence farming on Lewis and Stornoway. Little remains of his work other than a few scattered ruins, but the people of South Harris, unlike their northern neighbours, welcomed Leverhulme's plans and supported his endeavours.

For a brief time, the tiny harbour at Leverburgh flourished, busy with development schemes and expanding fishing activity. Sadly, because of financial constraints, Leverhulme was forced to curtail his plans. The turning point came when the Scottish Office refused to contribute a requested £100,000 towards the costs of Leverhulme's proposals, in spite of the fact that he had already, personally, spent upwards of one million pounds improving island life. Government

support for the Hebrides, before Leverhulme, amounted to a grudging £35,000 a year!

The A859 passes over the Obbe, dividing it from a fine salmon and sea-trout system: Loch Steisevat, joined by Atha Dubh burn to Loch na Moracha. A minor road follows the east shoreline, out to the Harris Loch Langavat, then twists southwards across the moorlands to Ardvey on the east coast.

Myriad small lochans between Langavat and the sea pin-point Braig-nam-bagh blue and silver over hundreds of acres and fishing in them for brown trout may be obtained through the Borve Estate office. The Estate and the Rodel Hotel also sometimes offer salmon and sea-trout fishing on the Obbe System.

I stopped for petrol in the village. The pump was operated by hand and I asked the owner about fishing the Obbe: 'Oh, just you go and have a cast for an hour or so. The upper loch fishes best and no one will bother you!' I politely declined.

Past the village school, on a flat piece of land overlooking the Obbe, is the local supermarket: 'These premises were built by the Highands and Island Development Board.' On the front door of the building was a notice concerning a public meeting regarding the issue of the moment – the prospect of Caledonian MacBrayne operating their ferries on Sundays.

This proposal has recently aroused great passion in the Hebrides and drawn fierce opposition to the plans from throughout Lewis and Harris, and also from expatriates and visitors from all over the world:

> SAVE OUR SUNDAYS. PUBLIC RALLY ON TUESDAY 13 SEPTEMBER 1989 IN THE COMMUNITY CENTRE AT TARBERT AT 8.30PM. PUBLIC RALLY ON FRIDAY 16 SEP/ TEMBER IN LEVERBURGH VILLAGE HALL AT 8.00PM. PURPOSE: TO CONSIDER AND OPPOSE PROPOSALS BY CALMAC TO OPERATE SUNDAY FERRY SERVICES TO THE WESTERN ISLES. WE REQUIRE ALL POSSIBLE SUPPORT TO OBSTRUCT THESE PROPOSALS AND A LARGE PUBLIC PRESENCE WOULD BE APPRECIATED.

One hundred and fifty people attended the meeting at Leverburgh and not a single voice was raised in support of CALMAC's scheme. Mr Donald MacKay, secretary of the Lewis and Harris branch of the Lord's Day Observance Society, commented: 'We are looking at all possible avenues to stand against this particular move. I have never seen the community in Lewis and Harris so united and determined on an issue as on this one.'

Mr N. M. Maclean, from Stornoway, claimed that: 'Any Lewis person that would sail on Sunday or do any business, God would have a curse on them.' John Macrae of Lochs, meanwhile, attacked CALMAC in rhyme:

> The forces of evil
> Are in battle array
> To destroy the Sabbath
> Wherever they may
> But the Lord is the same
> As in days of old
> He wrecked an Armada
> With the might of His
> Storms.
>
> To defend the Sabbath
> Our duty is clear
> The Lord on our side
> Is a hearer of prayer
> We should resolve
> As Shadrach of old
> That we will not bow
> To their image of gold.

However, people in other islands of the Outer Hebrides welcome CALMAC's plans, including Benbecula's councillor, Ray Burnett who claimed that at a recent Ward Meeting, his constituents made it plain they would support the proposed extension of Sunday ferry sailings. The battle lines have been drawn and the fight rages furiously.

The road leaves Leverburgh, narrowing invitingly across a cattle grid, leading up Gleann Shranndabhal into Glen Rodel then down to the most southerly point on the Long Island, the small, wind/ swept hamlet of Rodel. Enigmatic Harris weather had suddenly decided to play fair again and as I parked by the harbour, the sun shone brightly from a near/cloudless sky.

The tide was out and two boats lay drunkenly against the quay: *The Britannia* and *The White Rose*. Overlooking the harbour is the Rodel Hotel, a grim, derelict/looking building, seemingly falling

Neatly stacked peat cuttings drying in preparation for winter at Cliasmol

apart at the seams but flanked by a few expensive cars. The hotel keeps the keys for St Clement's Church, which I wanted to visit.

I walked up the short flight of steps of the hotel and entered. Silence and dust greeted me. Eventually, a man appeared and told me that there were people already up at the church, or that if they had gone, then the key would be by the door. I quickly escaped from the dismal interior, back into welcome sunlight, and headed for church.

St Clement's occupies a dramatic position on a rocky knoll above the village and dates from the early sixteenth century; although there was probably an earlier church or chapel on the site many years prior to the erection of the present building, which is attributed to Alexander Macleod.

Alex must have had a fine sense of history, because it is probable that he built the church for the principal purpose of making sure that he had a final resting place, suitable to his 'high station' as a laird. Macleod began work on his own tomb in 1528 and it is one of the finest examples in Scotland.

Useful notes in the church tell visitors the story:

> The most ambitious medieval building on the Outer Hebrides, its plan is the form of a cross. The nave continues straight into the choir without any structural break and small chapels, in the form of transepts project either side of the choir.
>
> It is clear that the design of the church was much influenced by the Abbey Church of Iona. The building fell into ruins after the Reformation; repaired and restored in 1784 by Alexander Macleod of Harris. Unfortunately, the church was accidently set on fire in the course of this work and had to be repaired a second time in 1787.
>
> The great glory of the church is the tomb of Alexander Macleod in the south wall of the choir, constructed for him in 1528, although he did not die until about 1546. Carved in stone from Carsaid. At the top are glorifying angels which are placed above the figures of the virgin and child and two bishops.

> To either side of them are fascinatingly realistic representations of a castle and a galley, and at the bottom is the scene of a stag hunt; which is followed by the depiction of an angel and the devil, weighing the souls of the dead.

A plaque on the wall commemorates the restoration of the church: 'Restored for worship and to the glory of God by Katherine Herbert, Countess Dunmore, in 1873.' Other, more famous and more recent visitors, have been the Queen, Prince Philip and Princess Margaret, who signed the visitors' book on 17 August 1956. No doubt the late Alexander Macleod, soundly asleep in his magnificent tomb, was suitably pleased and impressed.

The church tower, because of the rocky, resistant nature of the hill, is built on a slightly higher level than the main building. I climbed the stone steps leading to the tower, and then ascended higher, up two flights of wooden ladders. Small, quartered windows at the top gave me a wonderful view over the surrounding countryside: green, fertile fields, sunlight and shadows playing over calm waters.

North from Rodel, nothing can properly prepare the unsuspecting traveller for the sudden shock of the wild landscape along the east coast of South Harris. I have seen the deserts and mountains of Arabia, the hostile plains of Eritrea and the desolate wilderness of northern Finland – they are insignificant compared to the inhospitable, stunningly beautiful east coast lands of South Harris.

It is almost impossible to conceive of people wresting a living from such a landscape; or to conceive of the unfeeling cruelty of the nineteenth-century lairds and factors who evicted them from their rich, western machair lands and deserted them here. The soil is so sparse that the dispossessed people could not find even enough depth to bury their dead, and had to carry them to Luskentyre, many hard miles distant over the moors to the west.

The hills are almost bare of vegetation; any small patches of soil are eagerly cultivated using lazy-beds. God knows what sheep find to eat. Small villages crowd round seashore inlets, fishing boats

*Duncan MacAskill,
94 years young,
Tarbert's oldest
shopkeeper. He has
proudly run his
business since serving
at Galipoli. On his
return he vowed never
to leave the island
again.*

securely moored, fore and aft against storms. Stark estate fences, broken and rusting iron posts, scar the moor. Dividing nothing from nothing. Keeping nothing in and nothing out. Pointless reminders of man's acquisitiveness.

In spite of these sad, angry thoughts, the magic of the Harris hills still manages to cast its spell; and as I wound slowly northwards through Finsbay, Ardvey, Flodabay, Manish and Geocrab, I was enraptured by the endless array of sparkling lochs, glens and mountains; and the vista eastwards, over the shining Minch to where the blue Cuillin on Skye lined the horizon.

Back at the main road by Loch Ceann Dibig, I felt as though I were leaving another world. A secret, silent place, distant, hard and uncompromising; and yet, in its own way, gentle, welcoming and secure. Where man's only enemies and man's only friends are the constant seasons and the long song of eternal winds, blowing forever across the green and gold granite hills.

Meavaig tractor — they start more easily on a hill

4
NORTH
UIST

The ferry terminal at Tarbert on Harris is ultra-modern and well organized. Parking areas are neatly white-lined, with traffic lanes curving towards the loading ramp. When I arrived, a friendly argument was in progress between the young loading supervisor and the driver of a GPO van, bound like me for Lochmaddy and North Uist:

'Willie, you're just a menace on the road, that's what you are.' 'What would you be knowing about driving? I was driving motor vehicles before you were born.' 'And your ticket is wrong Willie; that van is far too big for this ticket.'

A tape measure was produced and both men pulled and tugged over the measurement of the yellow van until agreement was reached and the argument amicably settled.

About a dozen cars were waiting and the ferry appeared on schedule. Mast-heads first, then the white superstructure and black hull. *The Hebridean Isles*, flying the CALMAC flag, with the Scottish Lion rampant in the breeze. Fluttering from the bow flew a white and blue St Andrew's Cross.

The iron-green loading ramp lowered, like the claws of a praying mantis, and the vessel disgorged its cargo of backpackers, visitors, islanders and articulated lorries. I started the engine of my car and was waved on board. Within minutes, the ship had completed loading and was threading its way back down East Loch Tarbert, heading for the Little Minch.

The island of Scalpay lay off the port beam; protected by Scotasay, Stiughay, Stiughay na Leum and Rossay. Bonnie Prince Charlie hid on Scalpay in the home of Donald Campbell, after the Battle of Culloden in April 1746.

As the vessel cleared the long sea-loch and turned south by Reibinish Point, she curtsied to the oncoming waves. Dip, rise and plunge. The tangled east coast of Harris, boulder-strewn and scarred by jagged bays slipped by. Over the hills, Hebridean weather played its myriad games: sunlight and shadow on Clisham; thick, dark clouds covering Beinn Dhubh.

A long, startlingly white wake flowed astern as our propellers churned through the green waters. Red buoys, marking lobster pots, bobbed by the rocky shore. Suddenly, the ship's alarm siren screeched a practice warning, sending children scurrying to anxious parents.

September showers swept in and I edged into a sheltered corner; and found myself saying hello again to my tall hiking friend, also Uist-bound. We swapped stories and impressions of Lewis and Harris and he told me that he was a student from London. His principal pastime and greatest delight was travelling and this Hebridean journey was his final fling of the year before returning to his studies.

I arranged to give him a lift to the North Uist youth hostel, his last port of call before making his way to Lochboisdale on South Uist, then home. We plunged and rolled past Rodel and across the Sound of Harris, guillemots and gannets shadowing our progress. A flight of shearwaters overtook us, hurrying low over the waves to some urgent appointment on North Uist.

As we approached the island, the way ahead seemed to present an unbroken, impenetrable wall; with the hills of North and South Lee rising almost 900 feet, and Eaval to the south, leaping 1,139 feet from the grey waters of the Minch. Madha Beag and Madha Mor, twin-islet watchdogs, guard the narrow entrance to Loch Madha. Madha is the Gaelic name for dog, and three scraps of wave-beaten rock crouch snarling below cliff-scarred Weaver's Point and Rubha nam Pleac.

The ferry threaded its way past light-topped Glas Eilen Mor, Faihore and Ruigh Liath, across a sheltered bay, bringing welcome respite from our stormy journey. Match-stick figures grew into sweater-clad seamen and the bustle of berthing and landing began. Mothers hurrying white-faced children to the open car-deck.

The gentle, ship-side graze of steel against timber; a diminishing throb of engines; thick male ropes, looped over dark iron bollards; cars and lorries key-twisted to life. Except one. I searched furiously through my pockets. No car keys. My friend stood amiably by as my blood pressure rose. I dashed back to the lounge and hunted under various tables. Still no keys.

As I explained to the crew member directing off-loading what had happened, my companion gave me a whistle; the miscreant keys had been lying in the boot — where I had covered them with various bits of jackets, rucksacks and coats. Relief all round.

North Uist is seventeen miles long by twelve miles wide but time and tide have shattered the island into thousands of pieces. Sea- and freshwater lochs twist and intermingle in a mad maze through peat-covered moorlands surrounded by gently rounded hills and rich, fertile machair grasslands which blaze with wild flowers in the soft Atlantic spring.

Loch Madha wanders round a coastline of nearly 200 miles, scattered with hundreds of little islands, the most important of which are: Flodday, Hamersay, Ferramas, Cliasay Beg and Cliasay Mor, Keallasay Beg and Keallasay Mor, Minish and Cnap Ruigh Dubh. Headlands finger the bay, probing east and south from the narrow road that winds northwards from Lochmaddy to Lochportain. Begging the sea to keep its distance.

Mobile at last, with the rain coming down in solid sheets, we bumped down onto the pier and drove past the white-fronted hotel which dominates the harbour. I remember a previous owner of the hotel, George Peart, telling me of his introduction to one of Lochmaddy's many characters.

One morning, soon after George had arrived, a small, weather-beaten figure appeared at the door: 'Good morning Mr Peart, I'm your dustbin-man.' George shook his hand and asked: 'Oh, is that so; and exactly what is it that you do for me?' 'Well you see, every Thursday morning I take the dustbins from behind the hotel and place them by the road. When they have been emptied, I take them back.' George thought for a moment and then inquired how much this service cost. 'No more than ten pound a week, Sir, and very good value it is too.'

Some don't start at all . . .

Cattle at Newtonferry

On further investigation, it transpired that the old rogue had never lifted anything heavier than a pint mug — and that only as far as his mouth. George politely declined the offer and said that he would be able to manage to do the job himself.

Lochmaddy is a tiny cluster of neat houses, clinging precariously to the bay, as though constantly surprised at having successfully survived centuries of turbulent Scottish history. The harbour once boasted upwards of 300 fishing vessels. Medieval pirates sought shelter and provisions at Lochmaddy during murderous forays in the Minch. Vikings called the village home; stroking dragon-headed, shield-specked longships through the broken Hebridean waters to shores crowded with waiting women and ragged, cheering children.

The village is a quieter place today and is the main population centre of the island's 1,700 inhabitants. A primary school serves the needs of little ones before they are thrust into the world of secondary education at the senior school on Benbecula. There is a small hospi-

tal; a single church, the Free Church, ministered by the Rev. John Smith; a courthouse; a tourist information centre by the ferry terminal; and the village store, run for many years by Mrs Morrison.

The first time I called at the shop, in 1979, I noticed an antique glass-fronted display case on the counter, filled with cakes and bibles. God is alive and well on North Uist, and has been for more than 1,000 years. One of the most important religious sites in the Outer Hebrides is in the south-west of North Uist, close to the village of Carinish, just before the start of the causeway across the sands of the North Ford to Benbecula.

Teampull na Trionad, Trinity Church, was built by Bertrice, Prioress of Iona in the early years of the thirteenth century. Godfrey, Lord of Uist, confirmed the charter in 1389 and the Teampull was an important university for priests and the sons of clan chiefs. The church measures 62 feet by 22 feet and was constructed in stone faced with layers of small boulders and pebbles, much influenced by the Norse building techniques of the time. Of greater influence, how-

Drying the nets

The waterlogged Machair Sands at Clachan

'Look right, look left, look right again . . .'

ever, was Teampull na Trionad's most famous scholar, Johannes Duns Scotus (1265–1308).

Duns Scotus also studied and lectured at Oxford and in Paris where he argued against the Christian theology propounded by Thomas Aquinas. Duns Scotus maintained that theology was built upon faith, not upon theory. A practical man, a Scot.

The sad ruins of the Teampull where Duns Scotus spent his spiritual youth still watch over the tides that race to cover the shifting sands between Baleshare Island and Carinish; and the slow chant of the old monks may still be imagined in the soft whisper of wind round lichen-covered stones.

Nearby is a small, salt spray-swept graveyard, where the remains of MacDonalds lie asleep beneath clan-crested slabs, in eternal peace by the sea. Which is more than can be said for the unfortunate victims of the last great clan battle in the Hebrides. This was fought in 1601 between the ever-fractious MacDonalds of North Uist and the Harris Macleods. The fight took place near Carinish, adjacent to where the Old People's Home now stands and close to Johannes Duns Scotus' gentle church. The dead bodies were dumped unceremoniously in a burn, still known to this day as 'the ditch of blood'.

To the north of Carinish, a minor road leads westwards towards Baleshare island, joined to the mainland by a causeway over Traigh Sands. I turned right, before the causeway, and parked a few hundred yards up the road. 'Thanks, Bruce, I'll walk from here,' said my hiking friend. Across a green field, in solitary splendour was the youth hostel. A tiny, restored croft house, squat against the gales. My friend slung his pack over his shoulder, clambered over the wall and strode off across the field. We waved farewell.

North Uist is circled by the A865, a most convenient road which has one spur northwards to Newtonferry, the stepping-off place to the island of Berneray, which lies a few miles over a seal-bobbing sound. Although there is no record of Prince Charles Edward Stewart ever hiding on Berneray after Culloden, a more modern

Prince Charles, the heir to the British throne, 'hid' there recently, living the crofter's life, planting his potatoes along with the rest of the islanders.

The only difference with Prince Charlie's tatties was that when news of the Royal Spuds leaked out, a clamour of London hoteliers descended upon Berneray offering a king's ransom in cash for the product of our future monarch's labours. They should have known better. Nearly 250 years ago the people of the Hebrides refused a reward of £30,000 to hand over one Prince Charles and were hardly likely to accept modern blandishments of cash for the hard work of another.

Berneray's links with royalty go even further back than Bonnie Prince Charlie. Near to the town croft is the birthplace of Sir Norman Macleod of Berneray, a supporter of King Charles I of England. Macleod led a group of his clansmen in the royalist forces at the Battle of Worcester in 1651. Not quite the lost cause it must have seemed when they were defeated, Norman Macleod and his brother still had to flee for their lives. After the Restoration in 1660, King Charles II repaid the Macleods' loyalty by granting them knighthoods.

Berneray is a lovely island to visit, quiet and peaceful, with splendid beaches fringeing the west coast. About 140 people live here and their principal occupations are farming and fishing. Each year, from 16 to 22 July, there is a local 'feis' (festival) and visitors can find comfortable accommodation at the Crofters Hostel, run by the Gatliffe Trust.

The North Uist circular road is a sheer delight. Round every corner, over every hill, water sparkles, and to believe it you really have to see it for yourself. The island is an anglers' paradise and few other places in Scotland offer such a wide range of readily available sport to visiting fishermen.

Salmon run the Skelter system, close to Lochmaddy. Wild brown trout dimple hundreds of lochs with their busy feeding. Sea-trout leap and rush through the brackish waters of countless

Sporting gentleman's gentleman. Hugh Matheson

OVERLEAF *Otter country. Baleshare Sands at low tide can look deceptively firm under foot but it would be foolish to walk them without local knowledge of tides and quicksand*

voes and salt-water pools; and it would take several lifetimes to do proper justice to all the fine quality game fishing available.

The Lochmaddy Hotel is the principal centre of angling activity on North Uist and in its prime employed thirty gillies, sporting gentlemen's gentlemen. Now, the hotel is reduced to one and the glory days have gone; but what may be lacking in quantity is more than compensated for by quality. Hugh Matheson, the remaining gillie, is one of the best and finest fishermen any angler could ever hope to meet. A charming companion with outstanding skills and knowledge of North Uist game fishing.

Loch Scadavay is the largest of the North Uist freshwater lochs; an amazing array of headlands, bays and corners, flowered white with lilies, graced in winter by Icelandic whooper swans, covering an area of only one and a half square miles and yet with a shoreline that meanders fifty miles round the moors.

Hundreds of islands adorn Scadavay, reputed to number in total

A typical one-storey Hebridean house, unchanged for centuries, but now with double glazing

one for each day of the year and some of these islands even have their own little lochans. Brown trout abound. Red-speckled little beauties that fight like the devil. Ideal for breakfast, fried and dressed in island oatmeal.

Much of the agricultural endeavour on North Uist is carried on in the old way, and the main crops are oats, barley and potatoes. I glimpsed a smock-clad woman cutting yellow, wind-blown oats with a gleaming hand-sickle. No 'solitary Highland lass' of Wordsworth's fancy, but a robust, unromantic figure, busy with the everyday practicalities of wresting a living from the unwilling soil.

Clustered round many of the crofts are tumbledown sheds housing a few cows and farm implements; the inevitable, ancient, rust-red tractor, parked on a slope for easy starting. The peat stack, often as big as the house it heats, laboriously cut from spring moorlands and dried in long summer days. Warmth through unrelenting, dark, winter-cold months.

Meals on Wheels — the mobile grocery store

Collecting North Uist kelp for processing

OVERLEAF *Absolute peace and serenity, Blashaval*

Hens and geese squawk and squabble round the doors. Black-faced sheep ruminate by the roadside, staring at strangers with dark-eyed suspicion. But visitors are still greeted with the same Gaelic courtesy Dr Johnson experienced and described during his Highland tours with Boswell in 1773: 'Civility seems a part of the national character of the Highlands.'

The Norse name for the Hebrides, 'Havbredes', means the Isles on the Edge of the Sea, and the best farming land on North Uist, like its neighbours, is along the west coast. Sheltering from Atlantic gales behind high cliffs and golden marram-grass-covered dunes.

Few of the traditional 'black houses' remain; these sturdy, oblong homes of bygone days have been replaced by all-mod-cons semis and ubiquitous, mock stonefaced bungalows. The old black houses were rectangular in shape, some fifty feet in length and twelve feet wide. There was only one entrance to the house and the roof was thatched with turf and other materials which happened to be available: ferns, heather, straw and potato leaves.

Double dry-stone walls were built to a height of about six feet with the outer wall slanting outwards to ensure that rain dripped off, rather than seeping into the house. The space between the walls was packed with earth and rubble, making the dwellings surprisingly weather-proof and snug.

There were no windows and the corners of the building were rounded, to offer less resistance to the wind; a single hole in the thatch let smoke out, offset from the fire below to avoid rain dousing the flames. Animals and humans shared the same space and the fire was kept constantly aglow to provide warmth and comfort for both.

North from Clachan to Balranald and Hougharry is a superbly preserved croft cottage, nestling in the landscape as though it had grown there, rather than having been built. The land between the main road and the sea is a nature reserve where farming and wildlife live happily together. Close to the sea, by the crescent-shaped sweep of Traigh nam Faoghailean bay, is Goular, where the Reserve Warden lives.

There is an exhibition centre, housed in an old croft, where you can brush up on bird identification before venturing out into the sweet-smelling grass and marshlands of Balranald. The Warden will tell you which are the best places to avoid, where there are birds busy nesting, and which are the best places to view the many different species that call Balranald home.

However, no one can avoid hearing the rusty engined-grating call of the corncrake, incessantly filling the evening air, neck upstretched above the reeds, eternally aware of danger; his ungainly, startled, flapping, leg-dangling flight, in search of fresh cover when disturbed; the ponderous, nodding, old man walk whilst feeding. Deep in contemplation of his next morsel.

Balranald also plays host to one of Scotland's rarest birds, the red-necked phalarope. These lovely creatures arrive from Africa in May, to court and nest amidst the marsh and machair around Loch nam Feithean; feeding only at night, their slender bills probing lime-rich pools for molluscs and crustacea.

Other grand prizes await the ornithologist on North Uist. There are resident golden eagles, buzzards and hen harriers. Also, a good chance of seeing the magnificent white-tailed eagle, unmistakably dressed to kill in white head and tail feathers, sweeping the surface of the loch in search of unwary trout, or quartering the fields and moorlands for rabbit and hare.

Far more dangerous and rapacious animals swept the Hebridean moors during the sixteenth century; a time of almost constant warfare on the islands. Even after the defeat of King Haakon of Norway at the Battle of Largs in 1263, the Isles on the Edge of the Sea remained very much a law unto themselves.

The Lords of the Isles, Clan Donald, acted almost as though they ruled a separate kingdom, flouting the authority of Edinburgh during the years when Scotland was ruled mostly by regents and infant kings. The crown sat uneasily on the head of the monarch in Auld Reekie, continuously peering over his shoulder, afraid of the might of the Lords of the Isles.

*Bringing home the
peats on the road to
Clachan*

James IV was a boy of fifteen years when in 1488 his father was murdered. In order to avoid a similar fate, James played a waiting game with his unruly lords; cautiously eroding their powers, inch by inch, over a number of years. By 1493, James felt strong enough to tackle the turbulent Lords of the Isles and he confiscated the lands of the Ninth Clan Chief. Unfortunately, but with the best of intentions, he distributed the forfeited lands amongst the lesser lairds, chiefs and tacksmen, who immediately embarked upon a couple of centuries of general rape and pillage in their efforts to establish

Pobull Fhinn (Finn's People), an unobtrusive stone circle near Langass, North Uist

themselves at the top of the Hebridean heap.

It was left to James VI, 'the wisest fool in Christendom', to sort out the tangled, bloody mess. In 1603, after the Union of the Crowns, James sent Lord Ochiltree to the Island of Mull to secure the castles and provide a safe base for further action against his fractious, unwilling subjects. Ochiltree then invited all the Hebridean chiefs to a conference at Aros Castle, to discuss ways and means for bringing Hebridean violence to an end.

When the chiefs dutifully arrived, eager to air their grievances,

Ochiltree slammed them into the hold of HMS *Moon*, anchored conveniently nearby for that purpose. The chiefs were then taken to Edinburgh and imprisoned in the castle, there to stay until they came to their senses and signed an agreement that would ensure peace in the isles. Eventually, reluctantly, they signed.

The wealth of these Highland chiefs lay, not in material possessions but in the number and strength of their people. They were a warrior race, united under their chief, willing and ready to defend their lands and their rights, if necessary, by force of arms. There was hardship and poverty, but the clan looked after its own and the chief, although despotic, was father to all. For better or worse, the system worked.

It worked until the destruction of the clan system at the Battle of Culloden in 1746. The dilettante Young Pretender, Bonnie Prince Charlie, by his ill-considered, disastrous invasion of Britain, destroyed an ancient, established way of life and ushered in a new order that was to bring untold misery to the Highlands.

Under his rule clan chiefs lost their hereditary rights of jurisdiction and became simply landlords. Whereas before, clan lands were the property of all, they now became the sole property of the new lairds; and as these lairds became more anglicized, so their need for hard cash to support their altered lifestyle grew. This was to be provided in the form of rent and labour, either in kind or cash, and as the eighteenth century progressed, preferably cash.

An obvious source of revenue lay scattered round the shores of the Uists: seaweed. For many years, the islanders had used seaweed as a fertilizer, to improve the poor quality of their soil and promote better crop production. However, if the seaweed, kelp, was processed by burning to produce potash and soda, then this could be sold for use in the manufacture of soap and glass.

The industry was born in 1735 on North Uist and by 1812, the value of kelp production had risen to the not inconsiderable sum of £14,000 per year. Which was very good news for Ranald George MacDonald, the profligate, absentee laird. The estate was in the hands of trustees when young Clanranald came of age in 1809, having amassed debts of nearly £50,000 due to his high society lifestyle.

This wealth was produced for him by the islanders, who harvested the kelp, which Clanranald claimed as his personal property. Kelp sold for about £20 a ton and it took twenty-four tons of seaweed to produce a single ton. The islanders were paid a shilling a day in wages for their labour and, because of the system of land ownership, were forced by circumstances to work uncomplainingly for their laird's profit.

Even then, at the turn of the century, islanders were leaving to seek better fortune overseas in the new American colonies. This did not suit the laird or his factors because the production of kelp was highly labour-intensive. Every possible obstacle was put in the way of these wayward Uist men in their quest for a better life; and legal action was considered in their efforts to keep the crofters busily engaged filling Clanranald coffers.

The kelp industry collapsed in 1822, when barilla from Spain became more cheaply available and so the lairds looked to a new means for providing income from their estates. With the introduction of sheep to the north of Scotland, they found a possible solution: rent out the land as sheep farms to lowland farmers.

The only problem was the great number of people already renting and working the land now required. The solution was simple — remove the people — and the factors set about their task with alacrity, supported by the full weight, might and majesty of the law.

Alexander Mackenzie, in his masterly history of the Highland Clearances, written in 1883, described the plight of the people of Sollas, a village on the north coast of North Uist:

> Prior to 1849, the manufacture of kelp in the Outer Hebrides had been for many years a large source of income to the proprietors of those islands, and a considerable revenue to the inhabitants; the lairds, in consequence, for many years encouraged the people to remain, and it is alleged that they multiplied

to a degree quite out of proportion to the means of subsistence within reach when kelp manufacture failed.

To make matters worse for the poor tenants, the rents were meanwhile raised by the proprietors to more than double – not because the land was considered worth more by itself, but because the possession of it enabled the poor tenants to earn a certain sum a year from the kelp made out of sea-ware to which their holdings entitled them, and out of which the proprietor pocketed a profit of from £3 to £4 per ton, in addition to the enhanced rent obtained from the crofter for the land.

In these circumstances one would have thought that some consideration would have been shown to the people, who, it may perhaps be admitted, were found to be in altered circum- stances; but such consideration does not appear to have been given – indeed the very reverse.

In 1849, Lord Macdonald was determined to evict between 600 and 700 persons from Sollas, in North Uist, of which he was then proprietor. They were at the time in a state of great misery from the failure of the potato crop for several years previously in succession, many of them having had to work for ninety-six hours a week for a pittance of two stones of Indian meal once a fortnight.

Sometimes even that miserable dole was not forthcoming, and families had to live for weeks on shell-fish picked up on the sea-shore. Some of the men were employed on drainage works, for which public money was advanced to the pro- prietors; but here, as in most other places in the Highlands, the money earned was applied by the factors to wipe off old arrears, while the people were permitted generally to starve.

His lordship having decided that they must go, notices of ejectment were served upon them, to take effect on the 15th May, 1849.

When the people refused to move, Mr Colquhoun, the Sheriff-

substitute, arrived at Sollas with a force of thirty-three policemen from Inverness and brutally evicted the families from their homes. There was considerable resistance, principally from the women of Sollas, but to little avail. In 1850, the remaining villagers were also evicted, amounting to 603 people.

Macdonald's factor defended his actions concerning the evictions from his Hebridean estates claiming that he had been: 'prompted by motives of benevolence, piety and humanity; because the people were too far from church.' Alexander Mackenzie gave the laird and his henchmen a proper blessing:

> 'Oh God! what crimes have been committed in Thy name, and in that of religion? Preserve us from such piety and humanity as were exhibited by Lord Macdonald and his factor on this and other occasions.'

The other villages on the north coast were also cleared: Malaclete, Middlequarter, Dunskellor and Grenitote. Surprisingly, the village of Hougharry was spared and is now unique as it still retains the old shape and form of previous years.

North from Hougharry, to the west of the A865, is an unusual monument, dominating Loch Scolpaig. It is in the form of a crenel- lated tower and was built by Dr Alexander Macleod during the time of the mid-eighteenth-century famines, to provide work for the destitute people. At the same time, the Committee Road was con- structed across the north-west corner of the island, from Ardheisker to Botarua.

Beyond Loch Scolpaig, a track leads down to a delightful, sheltered, sandy bay, whilst a short walk north along the cliffs brings you the famous Sunken Caves of Hosta: deep chasms, filled with pounding surf and foam, torn from the crags by thousands of years of Atlantic swells and storms.

On a promontory near by, high above the waves, are the remains of a Pictish Fort, Caisteal Odair, 'the castle of the dappled hill'; and it is still possible to follow the line of the protective walls which

Sunset over Ahmore Strand

barred access to the rocky fortress.

Access to Vallay Island, north from Scolpaig, is less difficult, although great care should be taken to establish the route across the sands and tide times before setting out. Otherwise, you might have a longer wait on the island that you anticipated. However, this would be no great hardship, because Vallay is one of the world's special places: tranquil, serene and blessed with glorious beaches where you may laze away long summer days, disturbed only by the slow sound of the sea and the twittering of soaring larks.

The house on Vallay Island was built by Dr Erskine Beveridge, who wrote extensively on North Uist's prehistoric remains, in his book *North Uist: its Archaeology and Topography*, published in 1911, and now sadly out of print. North Uist is rich with prehistoric monuments: wheelhouses, chambered cairns and standing stones.

The most dramatic of these is the chambered cairn on the north slopes of Ben Langass, between Lochmaddy and Clachan. A huge pile of stones, measuring eighty feet in diameter, and rising to a height of fourteen feet. On the east side, a narrow passage leads to the central chamber where pottery fragments and arrow-heads were found.

Even more dramatic finds were made on Eilean-an-Tighe, an island in Loch nan Geireann, east of Sollas. The island is named on the Ordanance Survey map as Aird Reamhar and archaeologists have uncovered evidence of what may best be described as a 'pottery factory'. So much was found that it is likely that the pottery was exported, certainly throughout the Hebrides and perhaps also to mainland Scotland.

But for me, what lies in the waters surrounding Eilean-an-Tighe is of greater interest, because Loch nan Geireann is one of the finest fishing lochs in North Uist. Here, the angler will find the best of all worlds: free-rising wild brown trout that vary in size from three-to-the-pound, right up to fish of 4lb and more; and also sea-liced salmon and sparkling sea-trout, fresh from the Atlantic.

Above all, and far more important, there is absolute peace amidst glorious surroundings: soaring eagles, divers and curlew. The loch outlets northwards then winds across shining white sands to reach the sea past the island of Oronsay and the long finger of Corran Aird a' Mhorain.

With care and guidance, at low tide, it is possible to walk over these sands to a wonderful sea-pool, where Clett and Rubha Glas form a barrier to the returning Atlantic. A natural rocky breakwater holds back the foam-flecked breakers, forming a sheltered, seaweed-fringed pool. Crystal-clear waters reflect all the colour of sands, clouds and sky: green, emerald, silver, blue and gold.

Salmon and sea-trout, shining bars of pure silver surge in with the tide, leaping and splashing in endless, heart-stopping display. If North Uist means anything to me, then the evening view of Geireann sea-pool is my dearest thought. A memory that brightens the darkest hour, filling my mind and heart with hope and beauty.

5
ST KILDA

The islands of St Kilda lie 112 miles out into the wild Atlantic and forty miles west of North Uist. They form the rim of an extinct volcano, born sixty million years ago from the vast upheaval of tertiary explosions that shook what was to become Northern Scotland.

There are four principal islands: Hirta, 1,575 acres, where the St Kildans lived; Dun, a narrow rock-finger, rising to 570 feet, protecting Village Bay; Soay, 244 acres, off the north-west coast; and Boreray, 189 acres in extent and four, turbulent, dangerous sea-miles north-east from Hirta.

Stark, pinnacle stacks surround these awesome isles: Levenish, guarding Village Bay on Hirta; Soay's Stac Biorach (the Pointed Stack) 420 feet high; Soay Stac and Stac Dona, the Bad Stack, named so because it had no nesting birds. There is also Boreray's 'Warrior Stack', Stac an Armin, 644 feet; Am Biran and Rubha Briste (the Broken Headland); Rubha Langa and the magnificent Stac Lee, 564 feet (the Blue Stack).

Islands and stacks leap from the blue Atlantic in a nightmare tangle of storm-lashed cliffs that are amongst the highest in Europe. Conachair, 1,397 feet (the coming together of the hills) on Hirta, plunges sea-wards in a near-vertical drop. High peaks gather Atlantic storms; cloud-wisps and white mists, demure, long-skirted dames, shroud stark crags and green hills throughout much of the year.

Always, the relentless sea, surging in anger against black rocks, defying human intrusion, and the constant scream of the million sea-birds that call St Kilda home. Boreray hosts 50,000 pairs of gannet, the largest colony in the world; 63,000 pairs of fulmar nest on St Kilda; half Britain's puffins, 300,000 pairs; 15,000 pairs of guillemot; 2,600 pairs of razorbill and 7,800 pairs of kittiwake. These colonies were the principal source of food for St Kildans.

Birds cloud the skies, endlessly wheeling and plunging in search of food. Their droppings blanco-white the cliffs; marauding skuas and great black-backed gulls harry fledgelings and infant eider duck. The tiny, unique St Kilda wren (*Troglodytes troglodytes hirtensis*), pecks and hunts amongst the salt-spray, green-clad cliffs of Dun, shrilling spring and summer nights with its clear, sweet song.

Snipe whirr by ruined buildings in Village Bay; starling, collared doves and oystercatchers chatter and complain. Whimbrel, golden plover and curlew call from the steep slopes of Oiseval and Mullach Geal; wheatear, meadow and rock pipit dip and bob from hundreds of cleits, circular, stone-built structures used by the Kildans to store and keep dry peat, hay, turf, oats, barley, clothes and food.

Autumn and spring bring Arctic migrants: greylag and pink-footed geese and whooper swan, redwing, brambling, snow bunting, ringed plover, dunlin and sanderling. One hundred and thirteen different species of birds have been recorded on these lonely islands, including such Atlantic rarities as ruff, flycatcher and wagtail.

But without the vast colonies of sea-birds, gannet, puffin and fulmar, man could never have survived on St Kilda. They provided him with food for his family, oil for his lamps, shoes for his feet and profit to pay the laird's rent; and they did so, adequately for hundreds of years.

Neolithic man came to Scotland 4,000 years ago; trekking from Central Europe with his women, children, dogs and sheep. They settled throughout the north: in Caithness, Strathnaver in Sutherland, Orkney, Shetland and the Hebrides. Those who chose the Hebrides must have looked westwards and seen green St Kilda on the horizon; an inviting prize, seemingly offering good grazing for stock and island security for their families.

There is evidence of Iron Age settlements on St Kilda in Gleann Mor, a narrow, fertile valley on the north-west of Hirta, enfolded between the slopes of Mullach Bi (the Pillar Summit), and Mullach Mor (the Big Summit), and early settlers probably lived in Gleann Mor until the fourteenth century. Two streams tumble from these hills into the cold waters of Loch a'Ghlinne (Glen Bay): Abhainn

The village on Hirta where only dreams and memories remain

OVERLEAF
Village Bay guarded by jagged Dun

a'Ghlinne Mhoir and Abhainn Alltan (The Rivers of the Great Glen).

The best known monument on St Kilda is at Gleann Mor. 'The Amazon's House', home of the Warrior Queen, was named and described by Martin Martin, tutor to the children of Macleod of Dunvegan, the laird of St Kilda, who visited the island in 1697:

> The body of this house contains not above nine persons sitting; there are three beds or low vaults at the side of the wall, which contains five men each, and are separated by a pillar; at the entry to one of these low vaults is a stone standing upon one end; upon this stone she is reported ordinarily to have laid her helmet; there are two stones on the other side, upon which she is said to have laid her sword.

Fact mingled with fiction are the bones of Highland mythology and no doubt such a Warrior Queen did exist, but little is known of her exploits, other than her love of hunting and the scattered remains of her fortress home in wild Gleann Mor.

More substantial relics lie on the hillside above Village Bay: Iron Age hut circles; and the Earth House, north of the graveyard, a 36 feet long, underground tunnel with a flagstone floor, probably in use between 500 BC and AD 300. After these subterranean dwellings were abandoned, early islanders built domed houses, partly above, yet still partly under the ground.

The best example of a domed house is Calum Mor's House, just below the line of Head Dyke. It measures approximately 15 feet by 10 feet. The Rev. Neil Mackenzie, appointed minister in 1829, described these old domed houses:

> Of their most ancient houses several still remain. They are circular or nearly so, and roughly built. The walls are six or seven feet thick, with spaces for beds left in them. These bed spaces are roofed with long slabs, and the entrance from the interior of the house is about three feet by two feet.
>
> The walls are not arched, but contracted gradually by the overlapping of the stones to a nearly point. The entrance door is about three feet by two-and-a-half feet. The outside is covered with earth and rubbish and appears like a green hillock.
>
> In some places they are almost entirely underground. The furniture of these houses, so far as I can ascertain from tradition and what still remains, was a quern, a hollow stone for a lamp called 'clach shoilse', which was filled with oil, and a cinder of peat was the wick; a vessel made of badly-burned clay called 'cragan' which was used for a pot; a water-pitcher, a dish to drink out of and a rope made of hide.

Medieval houses were much more substantial and one structure still remains, west of Tobar Childar in Village Bay. Williamson and Boyd described it in 1966:

> The walls were of rough granite stones taken from the fields or pro-talus ridge beneath Conchair; the ceilings were formed of granite slabs laid across the tops of the walls; and so that the structure might have greater breadth, the long walls were cleverly corbelled, narrowing inwards from 7 foot apart at the floor to less than one yard at the top.
>
> The bed chambers were not hollowed out of the enormously thick walls as in Hebridean black-houses, but were tiny bee-hive shaped cells tacked on to the house, with a low connecting tunnel through which the inmates wriggled to their rest.

Prior to 1834, the St Kildans lived on Hirta in two rows of thatched houses, facing each other across a stone pavement known as the High Street. As elsewhere in the Hebrides, the corners of houses were not squared, but rounded, to offer less resistance to the mighty gales that swept round the dwellings, seeking to hurl them into the Atlantic. Thick, double walls were constructed, in-filled with soil to provide insulation, and there were neither windows nor chimneys. Timber beams were used to support the thatched roof and the

Village Bay locals

Only the islanders have gone — a view from a cleit on Hirta

whole thing was tied down using heath ropes, weighted with stones, or the long beaks of gannets, used as pegs. An opening was left in the roof at one end, to let light in and smoke out. A wall of stones divided the building into two sections: one for the St Kildans, the other for their animals. Manure was allowed to build up on the floor and the ashes of every fire were added and stamped into the pile.

R. Curruthers, in his *Highland Notebook* complained:

> Every hut is nearly inaccessible from the filth which lies before the door, consisting of putrid sea fowl and refuse of all disgusting kinds. The interior is scarcely better, consisting generally of two apartments; within one is the dunghill, gradually growing into a pile of manure, which is removed once a year to till the ground adjoining. The stench, both inside and outside is intolerable.

During the early years of the nineteenth century as increasing numbers of visitors arrived and explored St Kilda, they were shocked at the primitive living conditions on Hirta. Sir Thomas Dyke Acland, MP for North Devon, arrived in 1834 and left the Rev. Neil Mackenzie the sum of twenty guineas, to encourage the islanders to build themselves better homes.

Thus a new village was born and, under the supervision and encouragement of their minister, the St Kildans set about their task. The dwellings were constructed within the Head Dyke, enclosing an area of fifty acres. As appropriate for the deeply religious St Kildans, the church and manse were built first.

A crescent of thirty houses was constructed, but it still included room for the cattle at the lower end, with a drain leading out to the narrow strip of land each family cultivated. Neil Mackenzie then set off for Glasgow, with Sir Thomas's cash, to buy better furniture for the new homes.

But twenty guineas were not enough:

> It was necessary that I should go south to purchase the windows and other things needed for their completion. I soon

found that the money which I had was not nearly sufficient to purchase the things of which they stood in immediate need. I therefore went to Dr Macleod of St Columba's, and some other kind friends, and they entered so heartily into the matter that in a short time I had a good supply. . . .

The 'good supply' included: forty-seven bedsteads, twenty-four chairs, twenty-one stools, twenty-one dressers, twenty-one glass windows and various items of crockery.

In 1860, huge storms damaged many of the new houses and a subscription was raised in Glasgow to help the St Kildans and repair the damage. However, the then owner of the island, John MacPhearson, decided to build new dwellings and it is his row of sixteen cottages that visitors know today.

These dramatic changes to the St Kildans' 'quality of life', brought about during the period 1834 to 1860, were to have far-

Don't count on it

reaching effects on their future. For almost the first time in their history, St Kildans had to depend upon substantial outside help.

The 'improved' farming methods, introduced in all good faith by the Rev. Neil Mackenzie, increased crop production – barley, oats, hay and potatoes – but because of the lack of fertilizer and a proper system of crop rotation, the narrow strips of land they culti-vated became increasingly less fertile.

The new houses proved to be damp, cold and expensive to heat, placing great strain on the island's limited fuel resources. Valuable pasture was burnt as turf and expensive mainland coal had to be imported. The materials required to keep the old homes wind- and waterproof were in abundant supply on Hirta; the new houses required materials that could only be obtained from the mainland.

Perhaps even more damaging to the future of the community, was the slow realization that, in times of hardship, they could rely upon outside help to survive; rather than the old way, when they depended entirely upon themselves, their own resources and hard endeavours to wrest a living from the harsh Atlantic environment.

St Kilda had nearly always been self-sufficient. J. A. Mac-Culloch, in his *Description of the Western Islands of Scotland* published in 1819, commented upon the St Kildans' lack of interest in fishing:

> They possess already as much food as they can consume and are under no temptation to augment it by another perilous and laborious employment, added to which they seem to have a hereditary attachment [to sea birds as food].

Hirta supported good numbers of cows and sheep which provided supplies of milk, mutton and cheese. The sheep from Soay, descend-ants of the earliest sheep known to man, also provided wool for clothing, which the men wove in the long winter months. Shoes could be made from the necks of gannets; crops may have been meagre, but there was always enough to go round.

Above all, they had a never ending supply of sea-birds: harvest-ing them was their primary concern and principal occupation.

Julian Huxley described the St Kildans as 'the Bird People' and MacCulloch also wrote:

> The air is full of feathered animals. The sea is covered with them, houses ornamented by them, the ground speckled with them like a flowery meadow in May. The town is paved with feathers. The inhabitants look as if they had been tarred and feathered, for their hair is full of feathers and their clothes are covered with feathers. Everything smells of feathers.

Compared to many communities in the far north of Scotland and western isles, the St Kildans lived in comparative luxury at that time. Their tiny, sea-girt islands provided them with all they needed to sustain life. Nor were they hampered or harassed by the political upheavals of mainland Britain. St Kilda was a world apart; as long as it remained that way, then the islanders were secure.

But as the wind and the sea brought them good fortune in the shape of sea-birds and fish, so also, eventually, it brought St Kildans the sails and seeds of their downfall: increasing numbers of visitors, shocked by the primitive living conditions and, ultimately, the long, grey, humourless, intolerant, hand of the Free Church of Scotland.

R. Moray, in 1677, published *A Description of the Island of Hirta*; Martin Martin published the first extensive work about St Kilda in 1753, after his visit of 1697: *A voyage to St Kilda. The remotest of all the Hebrides, or Western isles of Scotland*. Thereafter, a succession of explorers made the stormy, dangerous passage westwards from Harris and returned to write stories of their exploits and of the strange island people who survived there by eating birds.

Buchan in 1752, *A Description of St Kilda, the most remote Western Isle in Scotland*; K. Macauly, 1764, *The History of St Kilda*; Lady Grange, *Epistle from Lady Grange to Edward D- Esq, written during her*

Soldiers waiting for the weekly mail drop

confinement in the Island of St Kilda; and from then on, the floodgates opened to an endless stream of Victorian and Edwardian 'reformers', all hell-bent upon improving the savage St Kildans. Savages the St Kildans were not, nor had they ever been. They were a deeply religious, Christian people and had been since the time of St Columba.

There was neither crime nor violence on St Kilda; no one man was owned to be better than another; decisions were taken by the whole community, in a truly democratic fashion; all in need were provided for — old, widowed, sick and lame. Triumph and disaster were the happiness and sadness of the whole village. They were healthy, revered their God, honoured their parents and adored their children.

This was in stark contrast to the lives led by most of the summer visitors who came to ogle and gawk in Village Bay. They came from a society riven by industrial and social disorder; where disease and disaster were commonplace. From a country endlessly pursuing Empire wars, steeped in dogma, conformity, class structure and the pursuit of double standards.

The St Kildans must have made those nineteenth-century visitors extremely uneasy. They were being asked to believe in the existence of a society, which was part of that Great British Empire, thriving under the most adverse conditions, not only largely unaware, but almost totally disinterested in their thrusting world. A family of people, living together outwith any need for formal or enforced law and order. Worst of all, to the Victorians, a happy society, seemingly without ambition, as they understood the meaning of the word, and without any need for the Victorian values of progress and money.

Something had to be wrong; and the church quickly discovered what it was: St Kildans lacked a true understanding of the Almighty. So it was the Church's duty, as Christians, to bring the islanders to a proper realization of their Godless state. The Church of Scotland began to take an interest in the St Kildans' souls, and

Delivery day. LCL in Village Bay

after the 1843 Disruption of the Church of Scotland, the break-away Free Church made the islanders into little less than slaves.

In 1697, Martin Martin found the St Kildans to be 'Governed by the dictates of reason and Christianity . . . and that the islanders were amongst the happiest people in the world.' However, this was not good enough for the Rev. Alexander Buchan who arrived in 1705, determined to: 'Root out the pagan and Popish superstitious customs, so much yet in use among that people.'

The Rev. John MacDonald, the Apostle of the North, began his mission to St Kilda in 1822:

> It grieves me to say, and I took pains to ascertain the truth, that among the whole body, I did not find a single individual who could be truly called a decidedly religious person; that is one who has felt the influence of the truth on his soul, and who exhibits that influence in his life and conversation.

From then on successive missionaries and ministers to St Kilda,

The old school room, Village Bay

Dramatic rocks on Dun

largely fed and sustained by the islanders' labours, had a captive audience and some acted as though they were God incarnate themselves. Few more so than the Rev. John Mackay who held the dwindling population of the island to holy ransom from 1866 until 1891; dishing out a quarter of a century of unadulterated, half-baked bigotry.

John Sands, visiting St Kilda in 1878, described a St Kildan Sabbath under the Rev. John Mackay:

> The Sabbath is indeed a day of intolerable gloom. At the clink of the bell the whole flock hurry to the Church with sorrowful looks, and eyes bent upon the ground. It is considered sinful to look to the right or the left. They do not appear like good people going to listen to glad tidings of great joy, but like a troop of the damned whom Satan is driving to the bottomless pit.

Nothing was allowed to come between Mackay and his compliant flock. He would preach for up to seven hours every Sunday. There were also services on Monday and Wednesday. All work stopped, before and after. A once happy, fun-loving community were drummed and dragooned into a docile flock of dumb adherents to the wishes of a near-demonic religious lunatic.

And yet, the St Kildans always obeyed and are reported to have admired and loved their harsh preacher. But as the years passed, MacKay's love of God and the ever-increasing numbers of summer trippers, offering easy money and the few goods the islanders could supply, sapped the St Kildans will to survive.

In 1852 many islanders emigrated to Australia and a shipwreck in 1863 further decimated the population when seven men and one woman drowned. But most terrible of all was the high infant mortality rate – eight out of ten children died shortly after birth from tetanus. All this meant there were fewer able-bodied men available to reap the harvest of sea-birds and as the nineteenth century drew to its close, the life of the islanders was becoming relentlessly unsustainable.

With increasing dependence upon practical support from mainland Scotland and the money gleaned from summer visitors, also came a need for regular communication with that source of help. In times past, St Kildans were content to receive the laird's representative once or twice each year, bringing them seeds and taking back rent in kind: feathers for army mattresses, fulmar oil for city lamps.

But by the turn of the century, the most important events in the islanders' lives had become the arrival of tourist vessels in the summer, and trawlers sheltering in Village Bay during stormy Atlantic gales. The skippers of these boats brought welcome supplies of much needed food and letters from far-distant relatives and friends.

But for months at a time, because of outrageous storms, St Kilda would be completely cut off from all contact with the outside world; and when supplies of food dwindled, the spectre of starvation became a nightmare reality. Nineteen twelve was one such year, when the islands were isolated for four months.

This near-disaster prompted immediate action, not from government, but from a newspaper, the *Daily Mirror*. Within hours of receiving the news, they had organized a relief expedition, supported by grocers Sir Thomas Lipton and Sir Joseph Lyons.

Shortly thereafter, again organized by the *Daily Mirror* and supported by Gordon Selfridge, the London department store owner, a wireless transmitter was installed. Sadly, due to lack of funds to keep it in good repair, it didn't last long and was closed down in 1914. The islanders were once more thrown upon the mercy of the elements and charity of trawler skippers for communication with the outside world.

One method of getting messages to the mainland was first used by a party of Austrian sailors, from the *Peti Dabrovacki*, shipwrecked on the island in 1877. The crew of eight had been stranded on St Kilda and John Sands, a frequent visitor to the island, found the solution to their plight:

On the 29th January, the captain and sailors called on me and felt interested in seeing a canoe I had hewn out of a log. I had written a letter and put it into her hold, enclosed in a pickle bottle.

The sailors, glad of anything in the shape of work, helped me to rig her and put the iron ballast right, and to caulk the deck. We delayed launching her until the wind should blow from the North West, which we hoped would carry her to Uist or some other place where there was a post. A small sail was put on her, and with a hot iron I printed on the deck, 'Open this'.

On 5th February we sent off the canoe, the wind being in the North West and continuing so for some days. She went to Poolewe in Ross-shire where she was found lying on a sandbank on the 27th by a Mr John MacKenzie who posted the letter.

The St Kildan Mailboat was used frequently from them on, mostly by tourists, but often by the islanders in times of distress; and is still used today by residents and visitors. Postcards and letters are enclosed with money for stamps and the little vessels are launched into the stormy seas from a point below the green slopes of Oiseval.

The wireless station was eventually repaired and manned during the First World War when it attracted the unwelcome attentions of a German submarine on 15 May 1918. Neil Gillies was there:

We had 'phoned down to the wireless and we 'phoned down that the submarine was making for the bay [Village Bay]. He came quite close, to the point where you could have flung a stone into the conning tower.

It wasn't what you would call a bad submarine because it could have blowed every house down because they were all in a row there. He only wanted the Admiralty property. One lamb was killed. We had the sheep down at the shore at the time, they were lambing. All the cattle ran from one side of the island to the other when they heard the shots.

The shadowy sea-bird cliffs of Dun

The result of the attack was the installation of a 4-inch gun, to protect Village Bay, but war ended and it was never fired in anger.

After the war, life on St Kilda became increasingly unsupportable and the end was in sight. The island was eventually evacuated in 1930 costing the government £1,000. On the morning of Friday 29 August the remaining islanders gathered in their homes to say Family Prayers for the last time. Having made their peace with God, they left their bibles open on the tables, fires smouldering in the grates, and at 7am made their way down to the fishery protection vessel, HMS *Harebell*, waiting to receive them in Village Bay.

Neil Ferguson remembers: 'I went for a last walk round the village. It was weird passing the empty houses; it was just like looking into an open grave.'

The St Kildans' decision to abandon their unequal struggle with nature was encouraged by the island's resident nurse, Williamina Barclay. Winter 1929 had been terrible for the St Kildans and in April Nurse Barclay asked them to consider evacuation. They agreed, and missionary Dugald Munro prepared a petition.

The document signed by the adults, twelve men and eight women, was sent to William Adamson, Secretary of State for Scotland, by the skipper of a passing trawler and arrived at Westminster in May 1930.

Civil servants and accountants considered the request. It was estimated that, over the previous five years, St Kilda had cost the taxpayer £2,388. Health £1,642; Education £453; Agriculture £82; Postal Services £211. The matter was decided; evacuation was the only solution.

The government acted decisively and with as much humanity and consideration for the St Kildans' plight as their understanding of the situation allowed. Under Secretary of State, Tom Johnston, and General Inspector of the Department of Health, George Henderson, both visited St Kilda and were shocked by what they saw. Evacuation plans were speedily prepared.

The islanders were to be re-settled at Lochaline and Ardtornish, near Fort William, and at Oban and in Fife. Homes and work would be provided by the Forestry Commission.

For the St Kildans, their traditional way of life ended. Circumstances beyond their control and beyond their full knowledge dragged them unwillingly into the twentieth century; and few of them liked what they saw.

For twenty-seven years after evacuation, St Kilda was owned by the Earl of Dumfries, a keen ornithologist, who jealously guarded his island sanctuary, steadfastly refusing all attempts by exiles to purchase any part of it. When the Earl died in 1957, he bequeathed St Kilda to the National Trust for Scotland and they had the Ordnance Survey prepare an official map of the island.

But St Kilda was not allowed to rest in peace. In the same year the Ministry of Defence decided to establish a missile tracking station on Hirta, linked to the work of the rocket range on South Uist. Extending the pier in Village Bay cost £500,000. Money was no object.

Today, these outlandish islands are a National Nature Reserve, managed by the Nature Conservancy Council and are on the World Heritage List. Yet they are shared by men of the Royal Artillery, Royal Engineers, Army Catering Corps and Royal Medical Corps and serviced by vessels of the Royal Corps of Transport.

Now on Hirta there are inside toilets, running water, an exercise gym, electric lights, televisions, a pub, regular mail; all the trappings of twentieth-century society. Regular communication with mainland Scotland too. Where there is a will, there is always a way. Sadly, it came too late to be of any benefit to the peoples who had lived and struggled to survive on St Kilda for nearly 4,000 years.

Each summer, the Nature Conservancy Council organize working parties to St Kilda. Three of the old cottages have been restored and they provide accommodation. Ornithologists, archaeologists, geologists and botanists now haunt the crags and valleys of Hirta. Visitors to the islands are warned by the Nature Conservancy Council that they must be entirely self-sufficient:

> All equipment and food (including bread) required for your stay must be brought with you. 'Living off the land' on St Kilda ended in 1930. Space on military transport is often at a premium and this fact should be borne in mind when compiling your equipment lists.
>
> A margin of at least a week should be allowed for the possibility of your stay being extended due to bad weather and extra food should be brought accordingly.
>
> All visitors are directly responsible to the Warden in all their activities whilst on the reserve and should report to him upon landing.

The island of Dun still guards Village Bay, but a tortuous road has been built from the village up to the saddle of Cnoc Sgar (the Bare Hill). From there, the road divides, to two radar masts: northwards to Mullach Geal (the White Top) and south to Mullach Sgar (the Clefted Hill Summit).

At the junction, there is a zebra crossing and post-box. The road north also boasts three bus stops, run by the Otter Bus Company: a sign on one of the posts, marked Hirta – Dun Auto Company Bus Stop, was erected by soldiers, to while away workless days on Hirta.

Workless evenings are spent in the pub, the Puffinn, drinking, talking, waiting for mail, like soldiers the world over. The mail plane does a trial run over Village Bay first, to check wind direction and speed, then mail bags are dropped on Ruival.

The drop-zone was first marked by a post, to which the soldiers fastened a teddy bear. By the end of the 1970s the bear was in rags and had to be retired. A coffin was made and the bear now rests behind the bar in the Puffinn, marked with the inscription, W.O.E. Bear; he is exhumed on special, festive occasions.

St Kilda is still a busy place: 107 Soay sheep were 'evacuated' from their islands in 1932 by the Earl of Dumfries and now run free-range on Hirta, 200 remain on Soay, unattended, self-sufficient,

Although the island was evacuated in 1930, many of the inhabitants have returned regularly to visit their old homes

OVERLEAF *Main Street, St Kilda*

completely wild, and much studied. Over the centuries, the island- ers also introduced more modern breeds: St Kilda Sheep, with their four splendid horns; Old Scottish Shotwool; and, more recently, the Scottish Black-face and North Country Cheviot. A few escaped 'evacuation' and can still be seen on the islands.

The prehistoric ruins in Gleann Mor and Village Bay attract studious archaeologists and there are more than 140 species of wild flowers for visiting botanists to study. The astonishing rock forma- tions, stacks and cliffs draw geologists from all over the world, and in recent years, sub-aqua teams have begun to study marine flora and fauna round the St Kilda archipelago.

But the true joy of St Kilda is still its sea-birds: fulmars, gannets and puffins in their thousands. Now, as in days past, they remain the all-enduring memory of visitors of these distant, magnificent islands.

But there is also the story of the men and women who lived and loved and worked and died there. Their crowded graveyard and the hundreds of cleits scattering the hills, and the sad ruins in Village Bay are their memorial. These and the endless sound of the sea beating on the shores of their memories.

> When the storm howled and the ghosts danced in the air,
> We have often seen him alone sitting upon the high rock,
> We have marked him speaking to the white moon,
> And caught his notes in the breezes of the night.

6
BENBECULA

Of all the Outer Hebridean islands, Benbecula, 'the hill of the fords', shows greatest signs of change. Balivanich is the principal town and administrative centre for the Uists and for the southern islands of Eriskay and Barra. There was also an important aerodrome at Balivanich during the last war. In the late 1950s the Royal Artillery established their headquarters here to service their rocket range on South Uist, and this military presence has grown steadily ever since.

The airport, which is both military and civil, lies to the north of Balivanich, with connecting flights to Stornoway and Barra, Inverness and Glasgow. A constant, modern bustle that has brought a considerable degree of prosperity and comfort to the local community; including an excellent Naffi — a much patronized and well-provisioned shopping centre.

Although the military presence is very obvious, and not entirely welcomed by all, outwith Balivanich, the island still retains its great Hebridean culture and charm. The western shoreline is fringed with fertile, productive machair lands, extensively farmed and drained, edged by golden beaches.

Moorlands sweep eastwards towards the stormy waters of the Little Minch, slashed by fjord-like inlets, and scattered with ruined shielings of former days. Much of these lands are accessible by good tracks, which served the townships that flourished there in times past: Gramsdale to Flodda; Market Stance to Rossinish and Scarilode; Olavat to Druim na Glaic Moire; Kilerivagh to Uiskevagh; Hacklet to Grimsay.

The improvement of these eastern moorlands was carried out after 1820 when the kelp industry was in decline. The best kelp came from Benbecula; therefore, as long as there was some profit to be made, the laird required people to gather the seaweed and man the kilns. The islanders were rented land and encouraged to build villages in the east and improve the bleak moorlands.

There was a vast increase in the production of kelp during the latter years of the eighteenth century and the first two decades of the

nineteenth, which meant there was an urgent need to retain a suppli-
ant labour force to gather and process seaweed. Prior to 1805, Benbecula was divided into nine principal farming and stock-rearing
areas, stretching from the western machair, right across the island to
the east.

These large tracts were broken up and rented to islanders, but
care was taken to ensure that the land given was not enough for a
family to live on – without also working at the laird's kelp. Worse,
the use of kelp as fertilizer was prohibited and any tenant found
doing so faced instant eviction. As the fertility of the land declined,
people became ever more dependent upon the manufacture of kelp
for subsistence.

Eventually, when Ranald MacDonald, twentieth Chief of
Clanranald had squandered his fortune in London high society, his
remaining Benbecula lands were sold to Colonel George Gordon of
Cluny. The reclaimed moorlands, so painstakingly improved by the
labour of hard-working people, were turned into sheep farms and
the inhabitants, with little recompense, ruthlessly evicted.

Benbecula is linked to its neighbours, North Uist and South Uist,
by long causeways and access today is easy. But before 1960, getting
onto Benbecula from North Uist was not so simple. The only way
in or out was by means of a dangerous passage across the soft
sand-flats of the North Ford, five difficult, low-tide miles over constantly shifting sands. Few arrived on Benbecula dry-shod and the
journey was always hazardous, particularly during high tides of
autumn and wild, winter days.

The tide was full when I left North Uist for Benbecula, driving
south from Carinish past Clett-feora to the first causeway-link across
the North Ford. It was opened by the Queen Mum in 1960, and I
wondered if she had had better weather for her journey than I had
with me that day. Rain lashed down in torrents and I could barely
see more than a few yards ahead.

Eventually, for safety's sake, I pulled over and parked on the first

*Anything worth
eating?*

OVERLEAF
*Golden Culla Beach,
Benbecula*

Sad reminders of times past — within the army base at Balavanich

little island, Gairbh-eilean, waiting for the storm to pass before continuing. The road was awash and wind-whipped, white-crested waves threw salt-spray high above the causeway. A solitary car limped past North Uist-wards, headlights ablaze. We exchanged nervous grins.

Then, as suddenly as it had arrived, the rain passed and a contrary sun blinked through black clouds sending thousands of shadows dancing amongst dark stones. Crystal clear droplets clung to slim stalks of sparse grass, and on either side of the road, soggy black-faced sheep chewed moodily, their thick, grey coats sparkling with silver specks of water.

Two bridges along the causeway allow the green waters of the Atlantic and Little Minch to mingle and the force of their flow through these narrow channels gives a stark reminder of the problems confronting travellers before the causeway was constructed.

The old way over the sands started from North Uist at Bagh Mor in Carinish and swung south-east, passing between the islands of Caigionn and Eilean na h-Airigh; then westwards, to the south of Eilean Mhic Caoilte, crossing the main channel before meeting a track out from Gramsdale to the south of Trialabreck Mor. The final part of the journey took the track between the rocks of Crois an t-sleuchd and Sunamul, reaching dry land and Benbecula at the head of Bagh Cnoc nan Gobhar.

Ray Burnett, Benbecula historian, school teacher and district councillor, in his definitive book, *Benbecula*, records the impressions of a traveller in the 1890s, making the crossing from Benbecula to North Uist in the company of Father MacDougall, a local priest:

> Heading due north, we came at last to the north coast of Benbecula and the entrance to the North Ford. Never before had I seen a more forbidding looking spot: before us lay many miles of mud and water, interspersed with islets and black rocks and dark tangles of seaweed clinging to them.
>
> My companion pointed north-east and indicated the line of the path across the perilous ford. 'Do you see those two high

rocks out there looking like two sentinels?' said he. 'Well, the path lies in a straight line between here and there.

'It is about two miles in length, and a yard or two on either side of it means that you are in quicksands which immediately swallow any man, horse, cart, or trap that deviates from that path. From those two rocks out there, you have to pick up a mark to the north-west and proceed straight for that mark which stands at the other extremity of the ford.'

Turning to my companion I said: 'Have you ever crossed this ford, Father?' 'Often,' was the reply. 'I was lost in it one night as I was returning from a sick-call on the other side. It was a wild night and I mistook my bearings in the darkness.

'While I was trying to correct them, I lost my horse and trap in the quicksands. The tide overtook me and washed me away; but in the end I reached an islet out west there, and so remained until two men in a boat found me the next evening.' Then removing his hat, he patted his snow-white hair, and smiled whimsically as he said: 'It gave me this.'

At low tide, lorries drive out onto the sands to gather seaweed, still used as fertilizer, and humans join the hundreds of birds – curlew, redshank, oystercatcher – probing for succulent cockles and whelks hidden below the exposed, white, tide-ribbed sands. Some of the finest seafood I have ever had the pleasure of eating has come from these shores. And you work up a mighty appetite digging for it!

To the east of the causeway, a narrow, circular road leads round the small island of Grimsay, separated from the rocky bulk of unin- habited Ronay by the narrow straits of Bagh Clann Neil. Crofts and cottages cling to the shores and the inhabitants earn a living in the traditional Hebridean fashion, mixing farming with fishing and any other suitable employment that happens to be available.

A delightful summer afternoon walk starts from the roadside lochan at Rudhadubh on Grimsay, wending up the hill and over the moor to Loch Caravet. Craggy promontories crowd the way eastwards to Loch na Faoileag and the village of Baymore. Out of

Tangle time at Peters Port

the village, a track skirts the main road which eventually brings you back to the coast. A short walk south-west leads to the ruins of St Michael's Chapel, founded by the Prioress of Iona, perched on rocks overlooking the sea at Eileanan an Teampull.

Benbecula has many similar ancient churches and chapels, mostly built during the fourteenth and fifteenth centuries and the island has a long tradition of religious tolerance. Today, the Catholic and Protestant communities of the Outer Hebrides meet and mingle on Benbecula, living together in quiet harmony.

I followed the main road over the final, longest leg of the causeway and arrived on Benbecula close to the ancient standing stone on the left of the road. More modern Hebridean construction work was in progress, funded by a grant from the European Development Committee, improving the road near Loch Olavat. The garage at Gramsdale looked exactly the same as the last time I had seen it in 1984: closed and surrounded by rusting vehicles.

Wrecked and rusting cars are a feature of the Hebridean landscape. They appear in the most unlikely places; in fields as make-do hen houses, as half-sunken hulks, poking awkwardly from the middle of lochs. It is not easy to dispose of old cars on an island; although it is said that a newly-arrived army officer once tried to help solve the problem.

The story is told that he decided to establish a good reputation with the islanders by organizing a weekend wreck-collecting operation for his men; clear up the landscape and exercise his troops in the art of vehicle recovery. A public service funded by the Queen. He tried once — but didn't try again.

After successfully retrieving a number of apparently abandoned vehicles from various unlikely locations, on the Monday morning he found his office besieged by outraged islanders demanding to know who had 'stolen' their property. Cars that had been carefully preserved for use as spare parts.

A visiting USA fighter pilot also supposedly incurred the wrath of the islanders, not so long ago, when he illegally broke the sound barrier, by flying too low over the island. A multitude of compensation claims poured in, culminating, it is alleged, in one claim amounting to thousands of pounds; structural damage to property, breakage of windows and crockery, miscarriage of sheep and cattle and severe stress — total £42,385.65.

I drove through Uachdar, past Macleans Bakery, open daily, past ruined croft dwellings, cheek-by-jowl with modern bungalows. On my first visit to Benbecula, complete with family, we rented a caravan at Uachdar and I was interested to see that the site now seemed to be used as a DIY centre. There's progress!

As a family, we are all game fishermen, parental brain-washing, I suppose. But there were never any problems deciding where to go or what to do on holidays. The sight of the countless numbers of lochs and lochans awaiting our pleasure on Benbecula had everyone beaming with delight from the moment of our arrival. The Outer Hebrides offer superb game fishing and nowhere is it more readily accessible than in North Uist and Benbecula.

A short walk from our caravan, across mushroom-studded, cowpat-caked grass fields, lay Loch Dun Mhurchaidh, one of the best trout lochs on the island, known locally as Caravan Loch. Not only does this fine loch contain excellent quality, huge wild brown trout, but it is also noted for Dun Buidhe, a prehistoric fortified dwelling, occupied at the time of the birth of Christ and sited at the tip of a narrow promontory, fingering southwards from the north shore.

Richard Feachem, in his *Guide to Prehistoric Scotland*, describes Dun Buidhe:

> This is one of several insular duns on Benbecula the majority of which conform in shape to the outline of the islet upon which they stand. The dun was originally reached by a massive stone causeway leading out from the shore by way of another islet; but when the water level was lowered this stood out partly on dry land.

The fortified islet, measuring about 150 feet in diameter, is

A game fisherman's paradise — view across the north of Benbecula from Rueval to the hills of North Uist

surrounded by the debris of a wall now spread to 25 feet in thickness. Within this is a dun, formed by a ruined wall about 13 feet thick and measuring 30 feet in diameter.

We had splendid sport on Caravan Loch and explored southwards, into the old lands of Aird and Nunton, walking the moor, fishing Lochs Fada and Eilean Iain, also with its own island dun, and Loch Borosdale. North from Borosdale is a narrow, unnamed loch, where my son, Blair, caught his first Hebridean trout.

I can still see him in my mind's eye, running towards me along the crest of the hill to the south of the loch, clutching the fish, red-faced with excitement, yelling in delight. Which is more than I did that day. I didn't catch a thing, in spite of my best and most careful efforts – other than the back of my neck and an unsuspecting sheep – because strong winds made casting difficult.

Strong winds are part of island life and as I drove through Balivanich, a gale swept across the airfield from Beul an Toim, rippling the long grass by the side of the road. One wild New Year's night, when Blair lived in Balivanich, their neighbour, the army chaplain and a man of slight build, first-footed him.

In due course, the chaplain took his leave. Concerned by the force of the wind, and anxious for the safety of his friend, Blair looked out of the window, and in horror, saw the chaplain, crawl-ing homewards, on hands and knees along the pavement.

Blair rushed bravely out into the storm and struggled towards his neighbour. Clutching each other around shoulders and waist, they inched together towards the chaplain's home where Blair eventually managed to deposit his guest indoors; whereupon Blair hurtled dangerously home himself, mightily assisted by the wind pushing him back, stumbling and falling along the way.

When my son told me this story I raised a quizzical eyebrow; inquiring if it had only been strong wind, rather than strong spirits, that had placed them is such a difficult position: 'Crawling along on your hands and knees on New Year's morning because of a gale? And you expect me to believe that?'

Old homes and old ways die hard — one of the last surviving traditional homes

A gaunt, threatening, ominous military aircraft squatted on the runway as I passed; clad in depressing dull grey, black and green, port and starboard lights flashing like primeval eyes. As the road touched the shore at Calligeo, a pair of eider duck bobbed busily in the bay and I turned southwards, past the incongruous, box-like houses of the army married quarters.

Leaving Balivanich is like taking a giant step backwards in time. Hay-stooks, in neat self-supporting rows, lined a roadside field. They had been saturated by the recent downpour and drooped sullenly, murky-yellow, waiting for collection. A ruined binder lay in a rusty heap behind a drystone wall; like some giant, tangle-legged spider, recovering after a nasty fall.

The school bus tooted by, filled with bright-faced chattering, waving children. I stopped by the burial ground at Nunton; dark crosses marked the last resting place of generations of islanders, waiting in silent ranks for the last trump, guarded by the ruins of the Chapel of the Virgin Mary. Nearest the chapel, the crosses above the quiet sleepers were weathered black with age; further south, less dark; until there comes the spread of bright flowers, covering newly dug grassy mounds.

For centuries, Clanranald ruled the Uists. They trace their descent from Somerland, the first great Lord of the Isles. Somerland claimed Pictish origins and he was the most powerful of the twelfth-century Scottish chiefs. He married a daughter of Olave the Swarthy, King of Man and the Isles, thus adding the Hebrides to his domains; and departed life in true Highland fashion, being killed at the Battle of Renfrew in 1164.

The principal Clanranald residence was Ormiclate Castle on South Uist built in 1701, but the castle was mysteriously destroyed by fire on 13 November 1715, the day of the Battle of Sheriffmuir, when the Earl of Mar with a force of 9,000 Highlanders met a force of 3,500 government troops in indecisive combat. One of the casualties was Allan, Chief of Clanranald.

With her husband dead and her home in ruins, Penelope, Lady

A fishing tradition

Clanranald moved to Nunton where a fine new mansion was built – it still stands, close by the old chapel and burial ground. Clanranald had cautiously supported the Stewart claim to the British throne and when the Young Pretender raised his standard at Glenfinnan, at the head of Loch Shiel in 1745, Clanranald men, mostly from the mainland, gathered there to raise a lusty cheer.

A few months later the carnage on Drumossie Moor at the Battle of Culloden ended Highland cheering for ever. Allan Ranald of Balfinly and Clanranald's second son, Donald MacDonald, lay wounded on the field of battle. MacDonald escaped, but Ranald, who could not walk, lay naked all night amongst the dead and

From the coastline of Benbecula, one can see the sun setting beyond St Kilda

dying, watching Butcher Cumberland's soldiers brutally murdering the helpless wounded.

Allan Ranald survived due to the humanity and kindness of a Captain Hamilton, who persuaded his fellow soldiers to spare the young man's life; but Ranald's injuries had been severe and he lived only a few years longer, dying at Kinlochmoidart in 1749.

Bonnie Prince Charlie, now a fugitive, then began that long journey through the Highlands and islands that has become entrenched in romantic Scottish history. But the real hero of the story was not the vain, ill-advised Young Pretender: the heroes were the countless numbers of simple, loyal men and women who helped and sheltered the Prince along his dangerous way.

Prince Charles Edward Stewart arrived at Rossinish on Benbecula on 27 April 1746; and news of the landing was quickly passed to the authorities in Lewis by a Presbyterian minister, John MacAulay. They quickly began assembling troops to search for the fugitive. Two warships and 700 sailors, commanded by Captain Scott and Captain Ferguson, the infamous, indefatigable Jacobite-hunter of HMS *Furnace*; and more than 1,500 soldiers under General Campbell.

During the following weeks the Prince and his party were moved round the islands: Scalpay, in East Loch Tarbert on 29

April; Stornoway on 5 of May; Loch Seaforth on 6 May; the island of Iubhard in Loch Shell in east Lewis, where they hid for four days; back to Scalpay on the 10th; Loch Uskevagh in Benbecula on the 11th; then Corradale, in the remote wilderness behind Beinn Mhor on South Uist on 14 May.

They stayed at Corradale in the 'Prince's Cave' for fourteen days, then returned to Rossinish on Benbecula, where Clanranald sent them food, clothing and wine. But as the hue and cry rose to a crescendo, Benbecula became unsafe and the Prince and his followers retreated once more to Corradale; where they whiled away the long summer days, fishing and entertaining visitors.

It is to the outstanding credit of the people of Benbecula and the Uists that the Prince remained undiscovered; almost certainly, everyone knew the location of his hiding place, and yet, even with the prospect of a £30,000 reward for information leading to his capture, not a word was said.

During his stay at Corradale, one of the Prince's visitors was Hugh MacDonald of Balshair in North Uist; it was a long, difficult journey over the most inhospitable terrain to see the Prince. Douglas Simpson, in his book, *Portrait of Skye and the Outer Hebrides* reports the conversation the pair of them had:

> I starts the question if His Highness would take it amiss if I should tell him the greatest objections against him in Great Britain. He said not. I told him that popery and arbitrary government were the two chiefest. He said it was only bad construction his enemies put on't. 'Do you know, Mr MacDonald,' he says, 'what religion are all the Princes in Europe of ?'
>
> I told him I imagined they were of the same established religion of the nations they lived in. He told me they had little or no religion at all. Boisdale then told him that his predecessor, Donald Clanranald, had fought seven set battles for his; yet after the Restoration, he was not owned by King Charles at court.

The Prince said, 'Boisdale, don't be rubbing up old sores, for if I came home, the case would be otherwise with me.' I then says to him, we would have no access to him if he was settled at London; and he told us then, if he had never so much ado, he'd be one night merry with his Highland friends.

There were to be few merry nights in the islands after Bonnie Prince Charlie's departure; by his actions he ushered in a cold, unfeeling harsh wind of change that was to sweep away the old Highland way of life forever. The perpetrator of this evil, however, then fluttered round the courts of Europe, descending rapidly into deceit and debauchery.

Eventually, with General Campbell at the North Ford and Captain Ferguson ensconced in the Clanranald home at Nunton, and after brief, ineffectual sorties to the island of Wiay, Rossinish and Calavay Castle in Loch Boisdale, the Prince returned to Benbecula. Lady Clanranald had devised a desperate scheme for the Prince's escape.

Flora MacDonald, then a young women of twenty-four, was the key to the plan. Her father had died when she was two and at the age of thirteen Flora had been adopted by Lady Clanranald. Captain Hugh MacDonald, Flora's stepfather, was guarding the South Ford and it was he who supplied the necessary travel documents which allowed the Prince, dressed as Flora's maid, Betty Burke, to escape over the sea to Skye.

Flora MacDonald was taken prisoner by Captain Ferguson and transported to Leith and then London, where after a year in prison, she was released under the terms of the Act of Indemnity in 1747. Her courage and demeanour in adversity so captivated the country, that upon her release she was presented with £1,500 by her admirers.

In 1750, Flora married MacDonald of Kingsburgh on the Island of Skye, and it was here that Dr Johnson met her in 1773, during his tour of the Highlands and islands of Scotland:

> We were entertained at Kingsburgh with the usual hospitality by Mr MacDonald and his lady Flora MacDonald, a name

*The airport on Benbecula has brought prosperity to the island, including the Naafi —
a modern shopping centre*

OVERLEAF *Causeway crash barrier on the way to Grimsay*

that will be mentioned in history; and if courage and fidelity are virtues, mentioned with honour. She is a woman of middle stature, soft features, gentle manners, and elegant presence.

The turmoil of the 1745 Rebellion left the Highlands devastated and leaderless, and succeeding years of oppression, rack-renting, clearance and eviction demoralized the people further. Only hope remained.

In 1883, a Royal Commission led by Lord Napier, travelled north to investigate the state of the Highlands. Based upon his report, the Crofters Act of 1886 was introduced, fanning an inextinguishable, land-hungry flame. Crofters were given security of tenure. The power and actions of their lairds, for the first time, were to be subjected to impartial scrutiny.

However, this did little to help those who had already been dispossessed and as the century drew to its close, more and more islanders began to take the law into their own hands: they simply raided, occupied and farmed the land their recalcitrant, absentee lairds refused to release.

After the First World War, with the battles fought and the glory won, soldiers returned from their nightmare expecting to find the government's promised 'land fit for heroes', with soil to work and homes for all. Instead, they found that the old order still prevailed and that the land they so urgently desired was to be left solely in the hands of the lairds.

They reacted violently. In 1922, much of Benbecula was owned by Lady Gordon Cathcart, an absentee landlord, resident in Bournemouth; and her factor, John MacDonald, was powerless to stop the land-raiding that was now concentrated on Nunton, the last remaining large farm on Benbecula.

By 1924, with the election of Britain's first socialist government, it was all over bar the shouting and the lands of Nunton were finally given over to crofting. A dark, black, despotic era ended; but the memory lingers on, amongst the ruined buildings and grey stones which mark the heart of so much hardship, toil and endeavour.

I looked around me, from my dream of these sad times, and found the sun shining brightly, larks singing wildly above and the sweet smell of seaweed filling the air. An old black and white sheep-dog trotted by, obedient behind a blue tractor. He paused briefly to mark his territory against a fence post, scraping his hind legs in quick triumph.

Turning west, I followed the road over the machair to the wide, shining sweep of Culla sands. The Atlantic rolled endlessly in as I munched a sandwich lunch. My children had splashed and swam here, on that first Benbecula visit. Me, safely at a distance, avoiding the look in my wife's eye that ordered me into the tepid waters.

The Gulf Stream brushes the west coast of the islands and sometimes, strange gifts are washed ashore: weed from the Sargasso Sea, coconuts and bamboo and even turtles. A loggerhead turtle was found alive in 1946 on North Uist; a leathery turtle in Loch Roag in 1985 and another at Ness, on Lewis, in 1987.

Less strange, though equally unexpected, creatures are sometimes found bathing at Culla; my son, Blair, reported a monstrous ritual, in which he confesses he took part. Swimming on New Year's morning, in company with a few demented, chill-less friends. A sure and certain method of blowing away last year's cobwebs.

South from Culla, behind a modern bungalow on the left of the road, stands the dramatic ruins of Borve Castle, built in the mid-thirteenth century by Amy, the first wife of the Lord of the Isles, and great church-builder of the Uists. The stones of the castle are specked green with lichen and grass covers the broken pinnacles.

There is one Benbecula name that almost rivals Clanranald in fame, and it is MacGillivray. I first noted the name more than twenty-five years ago in the pages of the magazine *Homes and Gardens*, where I read about a 'sale of Hebridean tweeds and tartan'.

The firm of D. MacGillivray & Co., 'patronised by Royalty and the Nobility' and 'Distributors for the Hebridean Crofter Weavers, Knitters and Craftspeople', began business at Muir of Aird, in a small house to the north of the road that links Peinylodden with

Hebridean autobahn, Carnan

Market Stance, south of Loch dun Mhurchaidh. Since then MacGillivray & Co. have prospered and expanded to a fine new building in Balivanich, where they service orders from all over the world.

The firm now offers an amazing range of high quality goods and services including: handwoven Harris tweed, camelhair, mohair and lambswool fabrics, clan tartans, Highland dress ornaments, dirks, skean dubhs, buckles, sporrans and kilt pins, walking sticks, handknitted sweaters, and stockings.

MacGillivray's even supply fine Hebridean perfume, handblended on the Island of Barra and invitingly named: Dark Glen, Plaid, Tangle, Caluna, Love Lilt, Moonglow, Melody and Legend. They also offer to organize your holidays and visits to the islands. Just tell them when and where you want to go and they will supply complete details.

A visit to Benbecula without a visit to the MacGillivray Emporium at Balivanich would be incomplete; and the shop is one of the most delightful I have ever visited, anywhere in Britain. They also carry a full range of island maps and information pamphlets, as well as a comprehensive selection of Scottish books – including, I'm very pleased to say, works by yours truly.

However, yours truly's most favourite place on Benbecula is somewhat more distant; far from the hustle and bustle of Balivanich business. It is to the east, beyond the gentle slopes of Rueval where Prince Charles Edward waited impatiently for Flora MacDonald so many years ago, across the wild, hotly disputed lands of Nunton Hill to Scarilode.

The track, which was originally a Clanranald kelp road, starts from Market Stance, the old centre of agricultural trading and cattle dealing on Benbecula; winding by Loch Ba Una, with its delightful, shallow, sandy north shore where we once had a memorable family picnic.

Just as memorable, although not so pleasant, was the experience of three Nunton men who spent a night in the shieling on the hill to the south of the loch. Late in the evening they were visited by three

Liniclate School, reputed to have the largest slate roof in Europe

strange women, who eventually turned into demons, leaving two of the would-be revellers dead and the third, narrowly escaping with his life.

The only demons we found at Ba Una were in the loch; superb little wild brown trout, in perfect condition, fighting fit, eager and ready to rise, even to the most inexperienced anglers' inexpertly presented flies.

The road twists on past Ba Una, through the moors north of Loch Hermidale, slipping silently between Loch na Deighe fo Thuath and Loch na Deighe fo Dehas; then swings south-east over the hill to the shores of Loch Scarilode and the old shieling by the sea at Oban Haka.

High banks surround deep blue waters; red-decked rowans cling to a small promontory by the shore; heather covers the hillside and the emerald green of former cultivation brightens the bleached yellow of sedge and deer grass.

In the 1940s Scarilode was still worked, the children trekking hard miles north to school at Rossinish. The last family left Scarilode just before I first walked down the narrow track to the loch in 1979; sorry to have missed them, but happy to have found a small piece of heaven.

Golden Eagle country. Eaval in North Uist dominates the northern vista from Benbecula. Between the islands lie hundreds of islets

7
SOUTH
UIST

The ford between Benbecula and South Uist is narrower than its meandering northern neighbour between Benbecula and North Uist. Because of this, the short crossing over the South Ford was always more dangerous. People tended to take chances with the tide, dashing across the sands at the last minute; and some paid for indiscretion and undue haste with their lives.

Creagorry, on the north shore, has always been a busy place and the Creagorry Hotel was well patronized by visitors waiting to cross the white sands. Ray Burnett recounts the impressions of John Francis Campbell, a gaelic scholar, who stayed there in 1859: 'A general air of listlessness about the whole establishment. Breakfast ordered at 8 — no sign of it until 10; but a capital place for stories.' In gaelic. When my wife and I paid our first visit, there was little evidence of any 'general air of listlessness'; the bar was brim-full of laughing people, no doubt all telling capital stories, but not being blessed with an understanding of gaelic, the stories remained the property of the tellers.

Other potential local property lined the shelves behind the bar: neat rows of brown paper bags, each filled with a half-bottle of whisky and two cans of export. Pre-packed carry-outs, to save time when time was called. The hotel was once noted in *The Guinness Book of Records* for the vast amount of 'water of life' consumed; and this tradition is alive and well today.

The causeway over the South Ford was completed in 1942 and is still known as O'Regan's Bridge, after the priest who was most active in encouraging its construction. It transformed life on the islands and provided a vital military link with the wartime airfield at Balivanich. The original narrow road was replaced in 1982 by a new, two-lane structure and I was half-way across it before I realized that this improvement has been made.

No one a-cockling today on the shifting sands of South Ford. Westwards, a long line of Atlantic waves whitened the horizon, rushing towards the black-ribbon causeway and their meeting with

The shell house, Eochar, South Uist, a famous tourist attraction

the waters of Bagh nam Faoilean which sweep in from the east. South Uist mountains, Hecla and Beinn Mhor, were shrouded in mist and I felt the nerve-tingle of excitement I always feel when arriving on this sweet Hebridean isle.

South Uist is about twenty-two miles long by up to eight miles wide. A single road, my old friend the A865 which I had followed down from Lochmaddy, runs the length of the western coast, ending at the pier in Lochboisdale. Lochboisdale is the principal population centre on the island, and was founded in the mid-eighteenth century when Gordon of Cluny evicted the people from their western lands.

First right after crossing the South Ford, at Ardmore, leads out through the straggling townships of Bualadubh, Eochar, Clachan, Linique and Kilauly, round the north shore of Loch Bee, to Ardi-vachar Point. The fine headland gives magnificent, uninterrupted views from Barra in the south to the hills of Harris in the north.

On the way back to the main road, stop at Bualadubh and visit the croft museum beyond the school, where there is an excellent collection of old farming implements and items of historical interest, including a scrap of material reputed to have been taken from Bonnie Prince Charlie's kilt. Were all the similar scraps of material from the Young Pretender's kilt throughout the Highlands authen-tic, then BPC must have arrived back in France bare-bummed and freezing, for they add up to dozens of yards.

Two miles south of the ford, past Ardmore, a minor road branches east, and wends tortuously over flat moorlands, past Lochcarnan with its unexpected jetty and power station, fingering southwards across a loch-specked landscape to Caltinish and East Gerinish.

LCLs, Landing Craft Logistics, flat-bottomed vessels that ser-vice the military garrison on the Island of St Kilda, pause at Lochcarnan on their stormy passage west. These uncomfortable vessels are run, not by the navy, but by the Water Transport Regi-ment of the Royal Corps of Transport.

The remote
wilderness of Beinn
Mhor where Bonnie
Prince Charlie hid in
1746

I served with the unit on the Isle of Wight in the mid-1950s, when the regiment was known as the Royal Army Service Corps and the vessels as LCTs, Landing Craft Tanks. In high seas, LCTs are one of the least pleasant means of sea-transport. Believe me.

Further south, past where the A865 is carried on yet another causeway over the emerald green waters of Loch Bee, the grander B890 also gives access to these wilderness western lands. It ends on the shores of Loch Skipport, the first of three long fjords that probe the rocky east coast of South Uist.

Loch Skipport is a favourite anchorage and picnic spot for the Royal Yacht *Britannia* on her autumn journey round the north coast of Scotland to Scrabster, to visit the Queen Mother's residence at Castle of Mey.

Loch Bee, known locally as two separate lochs, East Loch Bee and West Loch Bee, is a hugh expanse of shallow water which almost cuts the northern part of South Uist in half; meeting the Atlantic through the narrows at Clachan, and only prevented from touching the Little Minch by flood-gates at the head of Loch Skipport.

As I bumped by West Gerinish and Loch Duin Mhoir, bustling with tiny wind-whipped white horses, a familiar, welcoming figure greeted me: the statue of Our Lady of the Isles and Holy Child, to the left of the road on the west shoulder of Rueval. The statue was designed by Sir Hugh Lorimer and erected in 1957.

South Uist is a Catholic island and everything about the island seems to have a relaxed, tolerant air of quiet self-confidence, far removed from the sometimes frenetic gesturing of the Calvanistic north. I say this as a Scot, reared in the old Protestant way: hellfire and brimstone, twice every Sunday, from a small, crow-black figure in a vast pulpit.

High above the statue, on the summit of Rueval is a less welcome structure: the Royal Artillery rocket range firing point. I wondered what Our Lady thinks about the goings on of her fierce, war-like

Kelp is still collected on South Uist where it is despatched to Girvan on the mainland

neighbour? The road up the hill is in pristine, all-weather condition. Suppose that it wouldn't do to be late pressing the button. A long line of cars crowd importantly round the forbidding buildings.

The gem of these northern South Uist moorlands is Loch Druidibeg, a National Nature Reserve, cared for by the Nature Conservancy Council and covering more than 3,500 acres. The reserve was established in 1958 and is considered to be an outstanding example of the gradual change from heather-clad, peat moorlands to the gentle, fertile, coastal machair plains that fringe the western shores of the island.

The loch is a wild scattering of small islands, secret bays and promontories, drawing its strength from the heights of Hecla, a mighty monument of Lewisian gneiss rising to the south; the oldest rocks in Britain. The islands in Druidibeg preserve ancient, native, Hebridean woodlands: protected from the ungentle administration of men, sheep and cattle by the dark, acid waters of the loch.

Willow, rowan, birch and juniper grow in profusion; wild hyacinth, angelica, meadowsweet and royal fern abound. Greylag geese call Druidibeg home, living there throughout the year.

Those most lovely of all Highland birds, red-throated and black-throated divers, nest on the islands and by the shores.

But the reserve is not only a living museum; it is also a modern, working entity, demonstrating that man and nature can live in beneficial harmony – given the will. Druidibeg moor and machair blossoms into a glorious wild flower-riot of colour in spring, with wild thyme, clover, buttercup, daisy, selfheal, wild pansy, meadow rute, spotted purple and marsh orchids. The lime-rich machair are used for crofting, in the traditional way: livestock graze the rich machair during winter months and are taken out to the hills in summer.

Consequently, plant life flourishes, and the machair lochs provide an ideal habitat for waders: dunlin, redshank, snipe, ringed plover, oystercatcher and lapwing.

Heron and otter hunt the lochs; corncrake grate from shore-line reeds and marshy tussocks; corn bunting and twite nibble new heads of ripening oats and barley. Hen harrier, kestrel, peregrine, merlin and short-eared owl sweep over the silent lands in search of prey.

I followed the B890 eastwards along the north shore of Loch Druidibeg; mute swans, like white ghosts, serenely breasted the waves and I stopped by Glac a' Bhodaich to admire the view. Clouds cleared from Hecla. Afternoon shafts of sunlight slipped from behind the steep crags of Maoil Daimp, Coire na h-Eitich and Beinn na h-Aire; the sky turned light blue, edged with soft pinks.

As I watched the changing colours, a dark shape flung itself from Hecla's high corries: a golden eagle, soaring in the mountain thermals, its vast wings seemingly motionless, pitch black against the now gold and white sky. A second bird majestically appeared, and the two turned, wheeled and twisted in amazing display. I held my breath in wonderment; a moment of absolute beauty and certainty.

South from Hecla, the island rears heavenwards in a wild range of dramatic peaks, formed by the force of the massive geological thrust plane which created the Hebrides so long ago. Ben Corodale, breached by Bealach Hellisdale, leads down to the remote cave on the cliffs overlooking the sea where Prince Charles Edward Stewart held Hebridean court in 1746. The land then rises to the highest Uist mountain, Beinn Mhor, tumbling in ragged crags over Spin, Beinn Bheag Tuath west, and Ben na Hoe east, before being broken by the crooked finger of sea-loch Eynort.

The trackless hills of Trinival and Arnaval hurry southwards over Triuirebheinn and Beinn Ruigh Choinnich to the scattered mass of rock-fractured, island-clad Loch Boisdale; the last great South Uist fjord-sea-loch. Then the land gently folds into a wonderful, remote wilderness of hills and glens: North Glen Dale, Easaval, Garadh Ur, South Glendale, Maraval, Roneval and Hartabreak, with the shimmering waters of the Sound of Eriskay beyond, and a distant prospect of Barra.

My glorious golden eagles slipped behind Hecla and I retraced my steps, back to the main road and turned south; pausing to commiserate with a sad, single, bull, alone by the shores of a loch. 'What's the point of being a bull with no cows?' I heard him complain as I passed. The road is being mightily improved, with the help of Euro-money, and I fell in behind a huge lorry, loaded to the gunnels with seaweed.

Although seaweed is no longer processed on the island, it is still gathered and exported. Alginate Industries have a local manager who organizes the collection and the seaweed is despatched to Girvan, in south-west Scotland, where it is processed for use in making ice-cream, toothpaste, paper and as a dental material.

After carefully negotiating past the dripping load of Girvan-bound kelp, I found myself almost in the bank – the Royal Bank of Scotland. It was travelling along at a good lick, dark blue and bouncing. One forgets about the practicalities of finance in these remote islands and the travelling service offered by the Royal Bank of Scotland is much appreciated by both locals and visitors alike.

West of the A865, a number of roads lead out to the townships, crofts and lochs of the machair lands. One of the most famous of South Uist's sons, Neil MacEachan, a school teacher, was born at the village of Howbeg close to wandering silver Loch Roag and the shining sands of Bun na Feathlach.

Neil MacEachan was one of Bonnie Prince Charlie's most loyal and devoted supporters; and, after the Battle of Culloden, MacEachan travelled with the fugitive would-be king during all his long Highland and island journeys, rowing across the Minch to Skye with the Prince and Flora Macdonald, when his chevalier made the famous escape from Benbecula in disguise.

Neil eventually arrived in France where he married and settled at Sedan, and in 1765 he had a son, Jacques Etienne Joseph MacDonald. Jacques joined the French army in 1785 and quickly gained fame during the turbulent years of the French Revolution. In 1798 he was made Governor of Rome, and in 1809, after the Battle of Wagram, Napoleon elevated his Celtic general to the status of

Marshall of France and Duke of Taranto.

But Jacques Etienne never forgot his Hebridean origins and in 1826 made the long, difficult journey back to South Uist; where he visited his father's home at Howbeg and gathered up a box of earth and stones from his father's lands which he carried back to France. When he died in 1840, at Courcelles-le-Roi, the soft Uist machair soil joined him in his grave.

Less easy to remove from the South Uist environment are the inhabitants of the superb freshwater lochs: the finest quality wild brown trout in Europe. Along with hard-fighting, sea-liced salmon and Atlantic-fresh sea-trout. Sportsmen come from all over the world to fish on South Uist and sport is generally booked well in advance.

Captain John Kennedy, a Falklands veteran, is in charge of South Uist fishing and he knows the waters intimately. John may be found at the Lochboisdale Hotel, the angling centre of the island, or at his post office and workshop at the Bornish road junction on the

Looking towards Hecla and Beinn Mhor from Croic a Tuath

A865 by the slopes of Ben Corary.

John Kennedy is an expert angler and he specializes in constructing superb, hand-built rods. He also makes an amazing selection of local patterns of fly, all personally guaranteed to catch fish. There are a few patterns which he has devised himself over the years, based upon his extensive experience of South Uist fishing – including the Clan Chief, and the Tartan Fly – absolute certainties on any Uist water.

John is a friendly, approachable man, always ready to offer advice and share his knowledge with visiting anglers; and any visitor to South Uist looking for game fishing should make the pilgrimage to the Kennedy homestead, where he will be assured of a warm welcome and excellent directions about where to go to find the best sport.

South Uist is an island for lovers of the great outdoors: anglers, hill-walkers, climbers, ornithologists, botanists, archaeologists, geologists, and just simple, plain, beach lay-a-bouts. Days are never

Howbeg hens by Loch Fada

long enough for everything that has to be done, seen and experienced; and the most happy visitors are those who manage to combine an interest in all these activities.

I have had some tremendous sport on South Uist lochs; including a magnificent 3 lb trout caught in the shallow waters of Loch Stilligarry, whilst bank fishing one cold April morning. Well, to be truthful, I had become over-excited, seeing a fish rise just out of reach, and waded in; regardless of saturated shoes and stockings, damp trousers and the certain row I knew I was going to receive when I presented myself back home.

The west coastline of the island is graced by a long series of first-class fishing waters, many containing salmon and sea-trout as well as wild brown trout: Loch Bee, Dun Mhoir, Grogarry, Stilligarry, Schoolhouse, Roag, Fada, Altabrug, the Ollays, Bornish, Kildonan, Hallan and Dun na Cille. To the east of the A865 lie more, including the Barph System, flowing into Loch Boisdale, Fada, Cragavat, Stulaval, Mill Loch and distant Snigusclett, nestling between Arnaval and Stulaval, south from Loch Eynort.

All these waters are miniature nature reserves in their own right, graced by the inevitable mute swans, serenely studying your efforts. Flights of anxious mallard whisk by on urgent errands; heron stalk the banks, or stand, beady-eyed and motionless, dreaming of dinner. Curlew call from the moor and contentment is a tangible, living presence, embraced by the splendid solitude of the hills.

I turned west, following the little road out past Loch Vaccasary and Loch Ronich to Stoneybridge. Castle hunting. The track swings south, round the shores of West Loch Ollay and a few hundred yards past the loch, behind modern farm buildings, stand the ruins of Ormiclate Castle, the former principal residence of Clanranald, burnt down on the night of the Battle of Sheriffmuir in 1715.

Many years later, a descendant of Lady Clanranald visited the sad ruins of Ormiclate Castle. Wandering round the old stones, she noticed a flash of light in the grass; stooping down to examine the source, she discovered her ancestor's jewellery, lost on the night of the fire and supposedly destroyed in the blaze.

I followed the twisting road south between Loch na Duchasaich and Loch Tornish and at Bornish, turned right, bumping along the potholed road, skirting the puddles as best I could. The black ribbon of tarmac wound its way westwards over the bright, springy-green machair. Pockets of sand, like small golden pools, broke the surface of the turf.

Hungry seagulls circled eagerly over a dead rabbit. Sand dunes reared ahead and I bucketed out to Rubha Ardvule: a splendid promontory, poking into the Atlantic, graced with a small lochan. A pair of whooper swans, Icelandic visitors, bade me welcome. A gannet swept by in a flash of startling white, almost brushing my head with its black-tipped wings and I ducked instinctively.

A couple of fishing boats had been drawn clear, onto a man-made breakwater and causeway which lined the south side of the headland. A trig point and Second World War gun emplacement overlook the sea and I sheltered from the rising wind in its lee, counting more than a dozen spent shot-gun cartridges round my feet. Must be wildfowlers, shooting birds – the Germans have long since gone.

The machair plains flow north and south, edged by white sands that extend in an almost uninterrupted, twenty-two-mile long beach. For thousands of years, Atlantic waves and winds have deposited shell-sand along these shores, building up an amazingly fertile pasture which enabled generations of islanders to live in modest comfort and security.

Hundreds of families prospered on this rich coastal strip, until the terrible times of the clearances in the mid-eighteenth century, when their monstrous Aberdeenshire laird, Colonel Gordon of Cluny, evicted them to make way for sheep. The Uist clearances matched those of Strathnaver in Sutherland for brutality; people were hand-cuffed and dragged screaming to the emigration ships lying waiting at Lochboisdale.

OVERLEAF *Rocks resembling worn molars at East Kilbride. Months earlier a young whale had been washed ashore on these beaches*

Milking time at Ormiclate

In order to persuade them to go, in August 1851, Cluny's factor, Mr Fleming, commanded everyone to attend a meeting at Lochboisdale, warning that anyone failing to do so would be fined a sum of £2.00. He promised them, if they agreed to go, that they would be well taken care of in Canada; an agent would meet them at Quebec, they would be provided with food, shelter, clothing and money, and a guide would take them on, into Upper Canada, where there was land and work waiting.

The reality of the situation was very different from the glowing picture painted by the laird and his cronies. Alexander Mackenzie, in his great history of the Highland clearances, quotes a contemporary report from *The Quebec Times* which gave the true facts:

> We noticed in our last [edition] the deplorable condition of the 600 paupers who were sent to this country from the Kilrush Unions. We have today a still more dismal picture to draw. Many of our readers may not be aware that there lives such a personage as Colonel Gordon, proprietor of large estates in South Uist and Barra, in the Highlands of Scotland; we are sorry to be obliged to introduce him to their notice, under circumstances which will not give them a very favourable opinion of his character and heart.

> It appears that his tenants on the above-mentioned estates were on the verge of starvation, and had probably become an eye-sore to the gallant Colonel! What they were to do there? was a question he never put to his conscience. Once landed in Canada, he had no further concern about them. Up to last week, some 1,100 souls from his estates had landed at Quebec, and begged their way to Upper Canada; when in the summer season, having only a daily morsel of food to procure, they probably escaped the extreme misery which seems to be the lot of those who followed them.

> On their arrival here, they voluntarily made and signed the following statement:

'We the undersigned passengers per *Admiral*, from Stornoway, in the Highlands of Scotland do solemnly depose to the following facts: that Colonel Gordon is proprietor of estates in South Uist and Barra; that among many hundreds of tenants and cottars whom he has sent this season from his estates to Canada, he gave directions to his factor, Mr Fleming of Cluny Castle Aberdeenshire, to ship on board of the above-named vessel a number of nearly 450 of said tenants and cottars, from the estate in Barra; that accordingly, a great majority of these people, among whom were the undersigned, proceed voluntarily to embark on board the *Admiral*, at Loch Boisdale, on or about the 11th August, 1851.

But that several of the people who were intended to be shipped for this port, Quebec, refused to proceed on board, and, in fact, absconded from their homes to avoid the embarkation. Whereupon Mr Fleming gave orders to a policeman, who was accompanied by the ground-officer of the estate in Barra, and some constables, to pursue the people who had run away, among the mountains; which they did, and succeeded in capturing about twenty from the mountains and islands in the neighbourhood.

But they only came with the officers on an attempt being made on handcuff them; and that some who ran away were not brought back, in consequence of which four families at least have been divided, some having come in ships to Quebec, while the other members of the same families are left in the Highlands.

The undersigned further declare, that those who voluntarily embarked, did so under promise to the effect, that Colonel Gordon would defray their passage to Quebec; that the Government Emigration Agent there would send the whole party free to Upper Canada, where, upon arrival, the Government agents would give them work, and furthermore, grant them land on certain conditions.

The undersigned finally declare, that they are now landed in Quebec so destitute, that if immediate relief be not afforded them, and continued until they are settled in employment, the whole will be liable to perish with want.

SIGNED *Hector Lamont*
and 70 others

The Quebec Times report continued:

This is a beautiful picture! Had the scene been laid in Russia or Turkey, the barbarity of the proceeding would have shocked the nerves of the reader; but when it happens in Britain, emphatically the land of liberty, where every man's house, even the hut of the poorest, is said to be his castle, the expulsion of these unfortunate creatures from their homes – the man-hunt with policemen and bailiffs – the violent separation of families – the parent torn from the child, the mother from her daughter, the infamous trickery practised on those who did embark – the abandonment of the aged, the infirm, women, and tender children, in a foreign land – forms a tableau which cannot be dwelt on for an instant without horror.

Words cannot depict the atrocity of the deed. For cruelty less savage, the slave-dealers of the south have been held up to execration. And if, as men, the sufferings of these our fellow-creatures find sympathy in our hearts, as Canadians their wrongs concern us more dearly.

The fifteen hundred souls whom Colonel Gordon has sent to Quebec this season, have all been supported for the past week at least, and conveyed to Upper Canada at the expense of the colony; and on their arrival in Toronto and Hamilton, the greater number have been dependent on the charity of the benevolent for a morsel of bread.

Four hundred are in the river at present, and will arrive in a day or two, making a total of nearly 2,000 of Colonel Gordon's tenants and cottars whom the province will have to support. The winter is at hand, work is becoming scarce in Upper Canada. Where are these people to find food?

I stared moodily out to sea, puzzling over man's inhumanity to man; grateful that Alexander Mackenzie had so painstakingly and accurately recorded the grim details of these sad times for posterity.

I bumped back over the machair, past the football field and beautiful Bornish Church, built out of local stone, with its triple crosses: one on each gate post and the third above the main door. I carefully avoided two larks having a vigorous dust bath in a pothole and headed south again, past Flora Macdonald's birthplace at Milton, to search for the Kilpheder Wheelhouse which lies on the machair near Loch na Liana Moire, south-west of Daliburgh.

It took some finding, for there are no signposts. The small ruin is surrounded by a broken, rusting, barbed-wire fence and is typical of the many similar houses which must surely lie beneath the sands of South Uist. The Kilpheder house is circular in shape, rooms being formed by a series of walls, radiating from the central area. It was probably built about the time of the birth of Christ and occupied until the coming of the Vikings.

Evening was falling as I walked back to the car; Hecla and Beinn Mhor were clothed in gentle greys and blues; yellow tansy and purple clover blushed in the short sheep-cropped grass; peat-smoke drifted lazily skywards from white-washed cottages. Night came stealing in on dark wings. A late sheep-dog hurried homewards as I travelled the last few miles to Lochboisdale and supper.

The Lochboisdale Hotel greeted me with its customary hospitality and I made the pilgrimage to the public bar to say hello to South Uist's most famous ship: the SS *Politician*, a large photograph of which has pride of place on the wall. *The Polly*, as she was affectionately named by the locals, ran aground on Hartamul Rock, to the east of the Sound of Eriskay in February 1941. Her cargo included 24,000 cases of whisky and, rather than see them consigned to Davey Jones's locker, the islanders helped themselves, mightily.

Open on Sunday

'For peace comes dropping slow . . .' Loch Ceanna Bhaig

Our lady of the Seas at Garrynamonie. Gales have removed large pieces of the mosaic

The Polly was alive and well in the long bar and after supper I telephoned John Kennedy to find out where I would be fishing the following day; for I had decided that I deserved a break and that it would be little less than sacrilegious to leave South Uist without casting a line. In order to resist temptation, I had brought with me only the barest essentials: rod, reel, line and a few flies.

I awoke the following morning to find a huge gale blowing up Loch Boisdale. The waves were whipped white in fury and my heart sank at the prospect of struggling against the wind all day. Then it started to pour. Just my luck. Nevertheless, as we anglers say, 'You will catch nothing unless your flies are in the water,' so I set off to meet John at East Loch Ollay, where we planned to mount a furious assault on the salmon population.

The last time I had visited East Loch Ollay, with my wife Ann, she caught half a dozen nice brown trout and I caught half a dozen less; so, rather unkindly, I had renamed the water Loch Dam Ollay. Fates were much kinder that day. The rain stopped, warm Hebridean sun shone, and in an unforgettable agony of delight, I hooked, played and landed a magnificent, hard-fighting 8 lb salmon, silver and bright from its long sea journey.

I had been fishing with two flies, one of which was a local pattern, Charlie Maclean, named after one of the best loved and most respected of South Uist gillies. I met Charlie Maclean, shortly before he died, when I interviewed him for a book I wrote called *The Sporting Gentleman's Gentleman*; and I had mounted the fly as a mark of respect for Charlie.

The salmon was attracted by Charlie's fly, angrily grabbing the other, a Brown Loch Ordie. In the struggle, the Charlie Maclean was lost, fouled on a rock in the bottom of the loch. I was pleased that it had happened. It seemed to me fitting that the old man's fly should remain in South Uist, where he lived and worked for so many years.

John Kennedy caught a fish as well, so at about three o'clock, happy and content, we returned triumphantly to the hotel bearing the only two fish taken that day. Because I hadn't brought a fishing bag, I had used my briefcase to carry my lunch, reel, camera and all the other bits and pieces I lug around on my travels. So I received some strange looks from fellow guests, marching into the hotel, business briefcase in one hand, a salmon in the other.

My immediate problem was how to keep Fred, I call all my salmon Fred, frozen during the rest of my Hebridean journey and get himself safely home to Caithness. I wrapped Fred carefully in newspaper and popped him into the hotel freezer; making a mental note to remember to collect him before I sailed to Barra the following morning.

Well, the middle of the night really; for the boat leaves Lochboisdale at the un-godly hour of 0600 hours. So I paid my account after dinner and spent most of the night lying awake worrying about whether or not I would be up in time.

I was, and rose and dressed hurriedly, staggered in and out of the hotel loading the car; giving myself a pat on the back for remembering to put the snib on the lock to avoid shutting myself out whilst doing so. On my final trip, I grabbed Fred from the freezer and drove the few yards down to the pier where the vessel was waiting. The radio had broadcast severe gale warnings for the Hebrides and I wondered what lay ahead, in the dark, stormy waters of the Minch.

8
BARRA

I hunched freezing over the steering wheel in the dark devil-hours of morning. Wind buffeted the car. Rain swept knife-like across Lochboisdale. Barely half-awake, I watched in amazement as the level of the sea and the Caledonian Mac-Brayne ferry sank; and the loading ramp miraculously aligned itself with the jetty.

I gasped, grasping the wheel tighter. Then relaxed. The sea and ferry were not falling. The loading ramp was rising. An optical illusion, confusing my befuddled, early morning mind. The brightly-lit car-deck of the ferry seemed like the womb of an alien space craft. I would not have been surprised if the ship had taken off vertically, rather than nosing quietly out into the black waters of the Minch.

I was followed on board by a few other vehicles, including a large Island Council refuse disposal lorry; must be dustbin day on Barra. White faces peered suspiciously through rain-specked wind-screens as seamen purposefully clamped the wheels of vehicles to the deck, the sound of steel chains rattling in the darkness. Cold work.

Grabbing Fred, my by now frozen South Uist salmon, I stum-bled up the metal companion-way in search of the galley. A wel-come blast of warm air and the smell of breakfast cooking greeted me. I lingered gratefully, chatting to the chef who readily agreed to put Fred in the kitchen freezer for the duration of our journey.

As the lights of Lochboisdale faded astern, I peered through the gloom for a glimpse of ruined Castle Calvay, off the starboard beam, where Bonnie Prince Charlie hid from pursuers in June 1746. The storm sang through the rigging and I felt an unaccus-tomed twinge of sympathy for the hunted Young Pretender; which I quickly suppressed, remembering the havoc he had brought to the Highlands.

We rounded Rubha Meall na Hoe and met the long, sullen swell of the sea. Distant lights pinpricked the blackness, flashing their mariners' warning through the velvet night. Angry, white-crested waves rolled and tumbled us southwards past Rubha na h-Ordaig and Sgeir a'Mhill, the final South Uist stack by the jagged slopes of Ru Melvick.

I hoped our captain, unlike the fortunate skipper of the ill-fated SS *Politician*, would keep well clear of Hartamul Rock, and went below decks in search of porridge, bacon, eggs, toast and at least ten gallons of tea. Breakfast-time television blared unnoticed from a corner of the restaurant as the occupants concentrated on the serious business of reviving their cold bodies.

Feeling moderately more human, I returned top-side to watch the dawn. The island of Eriskay slipped by, a faint outline against the grey of the brightning sky. A flight of guillemots hurtled past, easily overtaking our slow, lumbering pitch and roll, their little wings going like mad. Must be late for school. Early-morning gannets, amazingly white, swept astern, shadowing our progress.

Through the gathering dawn, the hills of Barra began to form; the stub of Ben Eoligarry, rising above Isle Orosay; Ben Erival, Ben Verrisey and Grianan, sweeping up to Barra's highest peak, shapely

Heaval; flanked westwards by Ben Tangaval and the hills and cliffs of the islands of Vatersay, Sandray, Pabbay and distant Mingulay.

An almost mystical, magical Hebridean view. A dark line of islands, washed around by deep blue seas covered with white-topped waves, graceful dawn growing green and azure above them. Sunlight slipping from behind mountains, sending golden shafts glancing across the water. Grey layers of nimbus climbing the horizon.

Allt Heiker burn, sparkling silver, cascaded down Beul a'Bhealaich rushing to meet the sea at Earsary; a marker buoy, topped by two inverted red triangles, winked good-morning as we passed: six short, one long, every seven seconds. The Atlantic tide, flowing through the Sound of Vatersay to greet the Minch, threw waves into mad confusion as they assaulted the vessel from all quarters.

The green slopes and scarred cliffs of Muldoanich, towering 500 feet above the sea, guarded the entrance to Castle Bay. The sands of

Vatersay School in Vatersay Bay

Compton Mackenzie's last resting place, Cille-Bharra

Caragrich and Uidh on Vatersay shone snow-white in the morning as we slipped quietly between the protecting arms of Ben Orosay and Rubha Glas. Then, suddenly, in stark silhouette, the black walls of Kisimul Castle, ancient home of the Macneills of Barra.

Kisimul, dating from the twelfth century, has one of the finest situations of all Scottish castles, perched on top of a tiny rocky islet in Castle Bay, dominating the southern sea-ward approach to Barra. It is in the form of a square, enclosing a round tower and in its day was virtually impregnable, having a good source of fresh water drawn from a well contained within its walls. Uncompromisingly proud. Like its owners, Clan Macneill, who claim descent from Niall, High King of Ireland in the fourth century. There is a tradition that when the Lord decided to rid His world of troublesome men and instructed Noah to build the ark, Noah, being aware of the great importance of Clan Macneill, invited the chief to join him. Macneill replied, dustily, that he had a perfectly good boat of his own.

This must have been the case, for the Macneills of Barra survived the flood, and succeeding centuries, ruling their island kingdom until 1839. Even today, their descendents, when in residence, like royalty, proudly fly their flag from the castle tower. In times past, to emphasize their high place in the general scheme of things, a Mac-neill piper would climb the battlements of Kisimul Castle and announce to the world:

> 'Hear, ye people, and listen, ye nations! The Macneill of Barra having finished his dinner, all the princes of the earth are at liberty to dine!'

Macneill rule on Barra was paternalistic; very different from the harsh treatment so often dished out by less kindly clan chiefs on mainland Scotland. When a husband died, Macneill arranged for an alternative spouse; he found widowers new wives. If cattle were lost over the cliffs, Macneill provided replacements from his own herds. The old and infirm were 'adopted' and cared for by their chief.

Kisimul Castle was greatly damaged by fire in 1747 and the chief moved the principal family residence to a fine new mansion house at Eoligarry in the north of the island. But the collapse of the kelp industry in 1822 ruined the Macneills and the last clan chief, General Roderick Macneill, retired to London, hurt and bankrupt.

In 1839, his estates were sold to the infamous Colonel Gordon of Cluny, in Aberdeenshire, ushering in decades of hardship, evictions and emigration for the islanders; made even worse by successive failures of the potato crop during the mid 1850s. Many of Macneill's people were shipped, often against their will, to Canada, and Barra was largely given over to sheep farmers.

In 1915, Robert Lister MacNeil, a Canadian architect and descendent of dispossessed Barra crofters, successfully proved his claim to the chieftainship of Clan Macneill and became the 45th Chief. In 1937 he purchased Kisimul Castle and enthusiastically set about restoring the clan home to its former glory.

When Robert Lister died he was buried in the castle chapel and his son, the 46th Chief of Clan Macneill, is continuing with the restoration work begun by his determined father. Visitors to Barra during summer months may make the short passage from the pier to Kisimul and wander round the old grey walls, marvelling at the beauty and strength of this most ancient and lovely of Scottish castles.

As our boat nudged the side of the deep-water pier, seamen busily un-clamped vehicles whilst cold hands clicked cameras at the castle. I retrieved Fred from my friends in the galley and decided to follow Plan A: get Fred quickly into the Castlebay Hotel freezer, get warm, consume more life-giving tea, then explore.

A weather-beaten face appeared at the car window, asking for my ticket. I produced a long, multi-coloured strip, bitten away during my journey by successive inspectors; for some strange reason, not from top to bottom, but from the middle, up and down, seemingly at random. Nevertheless, excellent value. Known as a Hop-Scotch ticket. My journey, from Ullapool, through the Outer Hebrides and back to Oban on the mainland cost only £92.00.

The centre of the car-deck on the ferry acts as a turn-table and within minutes I had been whirled round through 90 degrees and deposited ashore. Ahead of me, the council dust cart, none the worse for its rough passage, was already busy emptying Barra bins.

I inched up the narrow road through the bustle of ferry traffic and turned left. Not much danger of taking the wrong turning or getting lost. I had seen the hotel from the ship, a tall grey building, standing above the harbour, a welcoming haven of comfort and warmth.

Barra is the largest of the southern islands of the Long Isle; approximately eight miles in length and six miles wide, circled by a convenient, narrow, twisting road completed in 1939. The islanders had to wait much longer for the benefit of electricity, which did not arrive until 1965.

Ensconced in the warmth of my Castlebay Hotel bedroom overlooking the harbour, Fred safely in the freezer, I unpacked and thankfully sipped a mug of hot tea. Castlebay looked exactly the same as the first time I had seen it: in the film *Whisky Galore*. It was shot on Barra and I imagined the enormous excitement that must have been caused on the island when this wonderful, enduring film was being made.

The author of *Whisky Galore*, Compton Mackenzie, was a founder member of the Scottish National Party and he came to live on Barra in 1928, at the age of fifty; by which time he was a well-known and established writer. A convert to Catholicism in 1914, Compton Mackenzie was greatly affected by the First World War, in which he served as an intelligence officer in the Aegean. In the small-scale and firm Catholic faith of Barra he found spiritual peace.

Mackenzie built a fine house on the north coast of the island, close to the white sands of Traigh Mhor, where Logan Air land their tiny aeroplanes – Highland and Islands work-horses. He also took a part in his own film, playing the role of the Captain of the MacBrayne ferry, and I delight in the twinkle in his eye every time I watch it.

I left the hotel, stepping out into the warm sunlight of the last day of September, and set off round the island, anti-clockwise, past the doctor's surgery and fine Catholic church – dedicated to Our Lady, Star of the Sea, which keeps Castlebay-time from a large clock on its tower – winding slowly up the steep hill over the east shoulder of Heaval.

Barra is traditionally named after St Finnbarr of Cork, or Saint Finnbarr, the gaelic monastic from Dornoch in Sutherland; or perhaps they were one and the same person? There is confusion over the exact origin. What is certain is that Finnbarr built his church at Cille-Bharra, in Eoligarry and that the site has been of great religious significance ever since.

I come from Caithness and like to believe that the man who gave his name to Barra was of Scottish, rather than of Irish descent. Alan Macquarrie, in his excellent booklet on Cillie-Bharra expounds the same view, supported by a translation of the Latin *Life of Saint Finnbarr*, extracted from the sixteenth-century *Aberdeen Breviary*; the only written Scottish record of the Saint and precised here:

> Finnbarr drew his origins from a noble Scottish family, from the island of Caithness, which branches off to the west of Scotland. A certain local king called Tigernach, who was of handsome rugged appearance, issued a public decree that no man should have pre-marital intercourse with any maiden.
>
> In spite of this a certain knight of the king's own family, by various means of persuasion, had carnal knowledge of a girl; and so she conceived a child and became pregnant. When the king heard her confession, he most wrongly and cruelly sentenced her to be burned in fire and sulphur.
>
> When the fire was burning fiercely, he ordered the young girl, who was pregnant with Saint Finnbarr, to be bound hand and foot, and thrown into the fire by the onlookers to be burned. But divine grace came down upon the fire and prevented its operation.
>
> The child Finbarr, still deep in his mother's womb, spoke thus to the tyrannous king and those with him, who shrank back in wonder to hear his words proceeding naturally: 'An unjust king, if it were right to call you king at all; rather, I call you an imperious tyrant. Why so cruelly do you condemn the innocent to the punishment that you have ordained for the delinquent, and have the just put to death along with the sinner?'
>
> Therefore he released the mother from her chains, and delivered her from death. When the child was born, he was baptized and given the name Finnbarr. Afterwards, having being instructed in the words of the gospel, he went to Rome, where after a short time he was ordained priest by the most holy father Gregory. Returning to Scotland, he converted many to the faith of Christ, and under his protection the reverend father Columba, long laboured in religion.

The 'noble Scottish family, from the island of Caithness' was most probably the clan Sinclair, whose ancestors had fought at Bannockburn with Robert the Bruce and died with King James IV on Flodden Field. Their name is remembered on Barra by Loch St Clair, also known as Loch Tangusdale, south from the sands of Halaman Bay and protected westwards by the heights of Ben Tangaval.

At the south end of the loch, on a small island, is a ruined castle; a broken tower, much like a miniature Kisimul Castle. Although its history is uncertain, it has been suggested that the keep was built by a Macneill as a home for one of his sons, who married a Sinclair girl from Caithness. The Caithness connection.

The best way to appreciate the beauty of Barra is to climb to the top of Heaval (1,260 feet), an easy forty minutes hike from the road. On the way up there is a dramatic statue of the Madonna and Child, made of Carrara marble, and from the summit you are rewarded with one of the finest views in the Hebrides.

On a clear day, the vista encompasses almost all of the Long Islands, from the mountains of Harris in the north, through the

Waves crashing at Borve Point, Barra

Uists, to the small isles scattered southwards from Barra: Vatersay, Sandray, Pabbay, Mingulay and Berneray. Barra hills are almost devoid of heather and are carpeted with wild flowers during the brief Hebridean spring.

Westwards, Barra's green machair lands are edged gold with superb, deserted beaches. On calm summer days, the whole island seems to rest in a shimmering sea of tranquillity, loud with the song of lark and meadow pipit.

As I came down from the hill, a brilliant fan of sunlight shone from beneath a low, dark layer of cloud. The waters of North Bay, Oitir Mhor and the Sounds of Hellisay, Fuday and Eriskay danced and sparkled in the clear air. Delicate shades of blue, pink, white and grey, spread over a vast masterpiece landscape of islands, sea and sky.

Continuing north, I passed groups of fresh-faced children standing by the roadside, clutching bags of books, waiting for the school bus; and I was engulfed in the morning rush-hour round Barra's single road; with at least half a dozen cars and the busy mini-bus rattling along behind me, stopping frequently to collect children and adults all bound for Castlebay.

An unexpected clump of trees clustered the roadside at Brevig. Not much future for trees on these windy isles; but they seemed to be surviving. A hydro-electric station towered by the shore, painted bright blue; and cycling furiously along the sands towards me, panting and pedaling madly, came a small boy. Late for the bus.

The usual Hebridean heaps of wrecked and dying cars littered the way; a rusting, bonnet-less, engine-less shell by the side of a ruined croft. I drew into a lay-by to let the school bus past and the children waved vigorously from the rear window. I waved cheerfully back.

Single storey houses cling to the shore. Not many multi-storey flats on Barra; nor much point in having a Rolls Royce or Bentley for that matter either. Nowhere to go. Other than round and round and round. A fishing boat lay up-turned above the tide near Earsary,

securely tethered agains the wind: *No. CY 136*. There seem to be more boats than cars on Barra, and certainly, given reasonable weather, it is probably faster to travel by sea rather than along the tortuous, grandly-named A888.

I noticed an old black house that had been carefully renovated and it merged into the landscape as though grown, rather than built. Four-rounded to the wind. Other, more modern timber buildings dotted the slopes, their red-pantiled roofs looking strangely out of place in such a wild setting.

A dour-faced postman passed by, un-waving, as I came to my first Barra loch at Ruleos. Barra is not noted as a game fishing centre, but it does have a few excellent trout lochs. On the moor between Ben Oba and Ben Verrisey, to the south of the road, lies Loch an Duin, full of bright little fish and the occasional sea-trout that climb the tumbling stream from North Bay. A dam has been built across the outlet and the loch is now the main water supply for the island, backed-up by tiny Loch Uisge on Cadha Mor above Castlebay.

Incredibly white, black-faced sheep chomped the short, hillside grass, remarkably fine, strong-looking animals, sturdy and fit; almost as though each morning their owners meticulously brushed and combed them before sending them out to pursue their never-ending, food-gathering existence. A single drab-white duck stalked pompously down to the sea for its early morning dip. I could hear it muttering 'Here we go again — and I bet its cold in there! But being a duck, what else can one do?'

A narrow causeway carries the road across the west shore of Bagh Hirivagh and I turned north by Northbay Inn. In the middle of the loch is a small island upon which stands an imposing statue of Saint Barr, mitred, his staff raised in everlasting blessing of the sea.

And poking sore thumb-like above the cliffs beyond the bay, a tall grey chimney marks the site of the factory where the results of Saint Barr's blessings are processed: Barratlantic Limited, fish and shellfish processors. Established 1974, an island co-operative, at the end of a weed-centred track, and doing well by the look of things. A sheep-dog bade me welcome to the factory, barking his head off from the confines of a small wooden shed. A tax-deductable guard.

I retraced my steps to the main road and followed my nose north to Eoligarry; a solitary rowan tree graced the banks of a bustling stream. Then, as a magician delights his audience with his magic, Barra dazzled me and held me speechless, breathless in wonderment at my first glimpse of the wide, white, sands of Traigh Mhor; backed by the high, golden grass-covered dunes of Traigh Eais.

A double rainbow arched over the dunes; rain swept by westwards. The waters of the bay were bright green and the contrast of light and colour was unimaginably lovely; defying description. An enduring memory for the dream-bank of the mind. A never-to-be-forgotten moment.

Dark sand-bags, built in a bund-wall causeway, marked the line of the old way over the strand, famous for its sweet-tasting cockles since 1594, when Dean Munro described them during a visit to Barra; and still sheltering in their hundreds of thousands beneath the smooth sands. Compton Mackenzie's house has been irreverently given over to the manufacture of concrete blocks and the processing the Barra cockles for the building industry.

The cockles are crushed and used as a beautiful harling on the facades of buildings; their broken facets reflect the light, sparkling and twinkling in endless delight; the rough surface is self-cleansing, channelling streams of rain-water down its jagged surface, washing every nook and cranny.

I stopped by the small airport building at the warning notice proclaiming: UNAUTHORISED VEHICLES ARE NOT ALLOWED ON THE AIRFIELD. A limp wind-sock was the only thing moving that morning and the tide was too far advanced to permit landing. So, taking courage in both hands, I defied authority and drove round to the front of the silent building, Port Athair Eilean Bharraidh, to take a photograph of this most remote and unusual of all Britain's airports.

The island narrows into a long peninsular north of the airport, and I edged round the eastern slopes of Ben Eoligarry to the end of the road, below Ben Scurrival and parked at the last house, over-looking the Sound of Fuday; a small blue-doored cottage with orange marigolds blushing shyly from behind a white-painted gate.

The island of Fuday lay before me; Gighay and Hellisay to the east; beyond Fuday, romantic Eriskay, love-lilting on emerald seas, with its two peaks, Ben Scrien and Ben Stack, clothed in wisps of clouds. Waves shone white against the cliffs of the Stack Islands: Eilean a'Gheoidh, Eileanan Dubha and Eilean Leathan.

Weavers Castle is a ruin standing at the southermost tip of Eilean Leathan; where an outlawed Macneill built himself a protective tower, from which he and his wife engaged in ship-wrecking activities, cutting the mooring lines of vessels anchored in the Sound of Barra. The Weaver and three of his sons were caught eventually and cut down themselves, permanently, thus ending their outrageous reign of terror.

Eriskay is where Bonnie Prince Charlie first set foot on Scottish soil, on 23 July 1745. He had hoped to gain the physical support of Macneill at Kisimul Castle but Macneill had prior knowledge of the Prince's intention and wisely made sure he was 'out' when the call came. Although a staunch Catholic, Macneill was in no hurry to join in such a mad adventure; and his caution spared his people much of the suffering experienced by the rest of the Highlands after the disaster at Culloden.

Coilleag a' Phrionnsa, the Prince's Beach, is on the west coast of Eriskay, backed by fertile machair grasslands. Tradition has it that the Prince planted a species of convolvulus, *Calystegia soldanella*, which he had brought with him from France, known to this day as the Prince's Flower and reputed to be unique to Eriskay.

I made my way back to Cillie-Bharra, and stopped to pay my respects to Compton Mackenzie, who sleeps beneath the green sward surrounding the old chapel. At the road junction in North-bay, the skies opened and rain descended in torrential sheets. The

OVERLEAF *A distant prospect of dreams. From the summit of Heaval, beautiful Kisimul Castle can be seen*

Bright boys from Vatersay School. 'Do you watch Neighbours?*' they enquired*

small wood in the glen below Ben Oba, proudly decked with sycamore, larch, pine, birch and alder, swayed drunkenly in the wind, and the outlet stream from Loch an Duin foamed furiously down-hill to greet St Barr in Bagh Hirivagh.

Lazy-beds criss-crossed the moor; damp cattle sombrely munched thistles; in a quarry by the loch, hungry machines chomped away at the hill to provide bottoming for urgent Barra road-works. I turned first right and followed the track northwards round Ben Cliad to Cleat: a few croft houses, clustering by a rocky shore. An angry-eyed sheep-dog watched me pass, then threw himself after the car, seeing me soundly off his territory.

Nestling in the dunes was a comfortable-looking caravan; by its side, a fishing boat, the *St Jude, No. 3285*. To my left, huge seas ended their long Atlantic journey, dashing themselves against the black cliffs of Cnoc an Fhithich. On my right, one of the most perfect beaches I have ever seen: a small crescent of footprint-less, shining white sand.

Northwards, endless waves rolled across the horizon, caressing the machair and sands to the west of the narrows of Eoligarry peninsula. I wandered, dream-like, across the beach, at peace with the world. Then it began to pour with rain again and I broke into a heavy lumbering, soft-sand-clogged run, heading for the cove at the far end of the strand.

I sheltered, my back against the black cliffs, waiting for a break in the weather; sandpipers danced a Highland Fling amongst retreating waves; the black head of a cormorant bobbed in the white billows; tiny rock-pipits hurtled onto the rocks above me at break-neck speed; it is as well they know how to stop quickly.

On my way back to the car, I found a mysterious, green bottle, washing back and forth in the tide. Eagerly, I picked it up, getting wet feet in the process, and examined it for any signs of a message; but it was empty. I searched my pockets for a pen and a scrap of paper: FOUND ON THE BEAUTIFUL BEACH AT CLEAT ON THE ISLAND OF BARRA, 30 SEPTEMBER 1988. BEST WISHES AND

KIND REGARDS TO THE FINDER. BRUCE SANDISON. I hurled it back, far out into the Atlantic.

Barra beaches are of outstanding beauty, and as I turned south, past Allasdale and Borve, clouds fled, sun shone and the day settled into warmth and light. Machair bordered the road, leading down to a succession of wonderful, deserted coves and bays, shimmering white by the blue sea.

Prehistoric man made his home on the west side of the island and the relics of his passing lie scattered in the glens and corries of Beinn Mhartainn, Ben Verrisey and Beinn na Moine: standing stones, chambered cairns, wheelhouses, duns, brochs and hill forts. From the security of their high island homes, these early inhabitants must have gazed in wonder at the fierce Viking longships, stroking carefully along Barra's rocky shores.

Similar security was sought more recently, for fugitives from another harsh regime; the late Shah of Iran sent his children to Barra during the last, anxious, dangerous, moments of his Imperial Persian rule. The family stayed at the Dark Island Hotel, overlooking the sands of Halaman Bay by Ceann nan Leac.

Almost, but not quite, so safe are the wild brown trout which inhabit Loch na Doirlinn and Loch St Clair, within walking distance of the hotel. As an angler, I found it impossible to pass by, in spite of best intentions; and I was glad that I had stopped, because these are two of the most lovely lochs I have ever fished.

Two hours bank fishing on St Clair rewarded me with a super trout weighing 2 lb 8 oz, a friend for Fred in the Castlebay Hotel freezer, and I missed three others which dashed savagely at my carefully presented flies. Later that evening, John MacCallum, a local teacher and keen angler, told me that Loch na Doirlinn has even larger fish, some of which weigh over 5 lb, but that they were very difficult to catch. I stored the information away for future use.

Back in Castlebay, I stopped in the friendly café by the harbour for lunch: a good Scots pie and cup of tea. Then walked down to the pier to catch the little ferry that plies regularly between Castlebay

Danger, sheep crossing

The peaceful machair sands beyond Vatersay Bay

Looking west to Borve from Heaval during the last dramatic hours of sunlight

and the island of Vatersay, twenty minutes distant across the shallow, green waters of Vatersay Sound.

The boat was crowded. A busy District Nurse, clutching urgent medical packages; the vet, off to minister to Vatersay sheep; three young, ear-ringed men, travelling home. And, most important of all, essential supplies for the islanders: six cases of whisky, neatly stacked astern.

Vatersay is famous for the 1908 Land Raid, when eleven Barra men took possession and started farming. The absentee landlord, Lady Cathcart, who had inherited the Uists and Barra islands from Colonel Gorden of Cluny, brought proceedings against the raiders and they were eventually imprisoned in Calton Jail in Edinburgh.

But the hue and cry that their detention aroused soon had them released and in 1909 the government bought the island from a much relieved Lady Cathcart and turned Vatersay over to crofting. There is little evidence today of these stirring times as I walked from the jetty along the broken road that leads to the principal township, two miles south.

Barra beaches are beautiful, but those on Vatersay defy description. To believe me, you really must see them for yourself. No words of mine could ever do justice to, or capture the serenity and outstanding loveliness of, these lonely strands.

High above the west bay of the narrow isthmus that pinches the small island, stands a sad monument to a ship that was wrecked there in the mid-1800s:

> 20th September, 1863. The ship *Annie Jane*, with emigrants from Liverpool to Quebec, was totally wrecked in this bay. Three fourths of the crew and passengers, numbering about 350 men, women and children were drowned and their bodies interred here. 'And the sea gave up its dead who were in it.' Revelations: 5:13.

South from Vatersay lie the uninhabited islands of Sandray, Pabbay, Mingulay and distant Berneray; once populated by crofters, but cleared over the years by their landlords, fate and changing fortunes. Sandray, which rises 640 feet from the sea, was farmed until 1934; in the same year the population of Mingulay abandoned their unequal struggle against the elements, leaving their towering, 800 foot cliffs to the sea-birds that had provided so much of their food.

It is possible to visit these remote islands today by chartered boat from Castlebay; and for those happy people who love the world's solitary places, there are few finer in which to search for peace and contentment. Vatersay itself is about to be brought into the twenty-first century. At a cost of £3.2 m a causeway is to be built, linking Vatersay to Barra.

The population of Vatersay has dwindled in recent years to less than sixty people and there are no single women of marriageable age left on the island. Mr Calum MacDonald, the Member of Parliament for the Western Isles said: 'It would have been a human tragedy if the Vatersay islanders were evacuated like the people of St Kilda in the 1930s, leaving their church, shop and crofts behind. That should never happen in the 1980s.' Thankfully, it never will.

Back in the Castlebay Hotel that evening, I celebrated the end of my Hebridean journey with sadness, but in style, with a splendid, farewell dinner: honest Scoth broth, crab salad, lobster and trifle, washed down by Chablis, followed by brandy and coffee.

After dinner, I sat by the window, watching the harbour lights, thinking of all I had seen and learned. Of Neolithic farmers and Viking raiders. Wild Picts and warring clans. Vibrant Stornoway and desolate Harris. The wilderness, watery moorlands of North Uist. Distant St Kilda. Lazy-beds and ruined croft villages. Gentle Benbecula and glorious South Uist. The magnificent islands of Barra. The lovely Hebrides, islands on the edge of the world.

Cille-Barra graveyard

SELECTED BIBLIOGRAPHY

ANGUS, S., *Hebridean Naturalist*, Stornoway Gazette, 1987.

BURNETT, RAY, *Benbecula*, Mingulay Press, 1986.

CHAMBERS, W. *The Story of Lady Grange*, Chambers Journal, No. 551, 1874.

CRUMMY, JOHN, *Hebridean Naturalist*, Peterborough Printcentre, 1983.

FEACHAM, RICHARD, *Guide to Prehistoric Scotland*, Batsford, 19863.

GRANT, JAMES SHAW, *Surprise Island*, James Thin, 1983.

LACAILLE, A. D., *Stone Age in Scotland*, Wellcome, 1954.

MACDONALD, DONALD, *Lewis: A History of the Island*, Gordon Publishing, 1983.

MACKENZIE, ALEXANDER, *History of the Highland Clearances*, Melven Press, 1986.

MACLEAN, CHARLES, *Island on the Edge of the World: Utopian St Kilda and its Passing*, Canongate, 1972.

MACQUARRIE, ALAN, *Cille-Bharra*, Grant Books, 1984.

MARTIN, MARTIN, *A Description of the Western Isles*, Mercat Press, 1970.

MURRAY, WILIAM HUTCHINSON, *The Hebrides*, Heinemann, 1966.

———*The Islands of Western Scotland: Inner and Outer Hebrides*, Methuen, 1973.

NAISMITH, WILLIAM W. and HODGE, E. W., *Islands of Scotland*, Scottish Mountaineering Club, 1952.

QUINE, D. A., *St Kilda Revisited*, Dowland Press, 1982.

SIMPSON, W. DOUGLAS, *Portrait of Skye and the Outer Hebrides*, Robert Hale, 1967.

STEEL, TOM, *Life and Death of St Kilda*, Fontana Books, 1975.

SUTHERLAND, DONALD, *Behold! The Hebrides*, Frewin, 1968.

THOMPSON, FRANCIS, *The Uists and Barra*, David & Charles, 1974.

TINDALL, JEMIMA, *Scottish Island Hopping*, Macdonald, 1981.

WILLIAMSON, K. and MORTON BOYD, J., *St Kilda Summer*, 1960.